The Executive Summary

The Executive Summary

A Commentary on the Gospel of Mark

MARK L. PELESH

RESOURCE *Publications* • Eugene, Oregon

THE EXECUTIVE SUMMARY
A Commentary on the Gospel of Mark

Copyright © 2024 Mark L. Pelesh. All rights reserved. Except for brief quotations in critical publications or reviews, no part of this book may be reproduced in any manner without prior written permission from the publisher. Write: Permissions, Wipf and Stock Publishers, 199 W. 8th Ave., Suite 3, Eugene, OR 97401.

Resource Publications
An Imprint of Wipf and Stock Publishers
199 W. 8th Ave., Suite 3
Eugene, OR 97401

www.wipfandstock.com

PAPERBACK ISBN: 979-8-3852-3132-4
HARDCOVER ISBN: 979-8-3852-3133-1
EBOOK ISBN: 979-8-3852-3134-8

12/03/24

Scripture quotations are from New Revised Standard Version Bible, copyright © 1989 National Council of the Churches of Christ in the United States of America. Used by permission. All rights reserved worldwide.

For Carole, Andrew, and Anna

Contents

	Introduction	ix
1	The Headlines	1
2	The Conflict Begins	6
3	Unclean Spirits and True Kindred	9
4	Teaching	13
5	Healing	18
6	Reprise	23
7	Gentiles	28
8	The Big Reveal	32
9	Getting Ready	36
10	On to Jerusalem	41
11	Jerusalem: Throwing the Gauntlet	45
12	Jerusalem: Routing the Establishment	49
13	Jerusalem: The Shape of Things to Come	52
14	Jerusalem: Passover	56
15	Jerusalem: Death	61
16	Resurrection	65
	Chavrusa	69
	Afterword—For Additional Study	73

Introduction

MY FATHER'S PLAN WAS to have four sons and name them after each of the gospel authors. I was the first-born, but his plan fizzled thereafter. (I have one sibling, and his name is Bill.) Nevertheless, this was probably the beginning of my affinity for the Gospel of Mark. As I grew up in the church and discovered an interest in history, I learned that Mark was very likely the oldest of the gospels. My appreciation for this type of historical source added to my interest. Mark is also—on the surface at least—more direct and fast-paced, appealing qualities to me as an advocate and writer. Indeed, Rev. Matthew Kozlowski, Associate Rector of All Saints Church, Chevy Chase, Maryland, described Mark in a sermon as the "executive summary gospel." Like a good executive summary, Mark's Gospel is relatively brief and presents the key points about Jesus. This all set the stage for me to try to delve more deeply into Mark.

A more immediate catalyst was being asked by the clergy at All Saints to author some of the short online daily devotionals sent to parishioners during the COVID-19 pandemic. I found inspiration from the Hebrew Prophets, the Psalms, and the Gospels, especially Mark. I have come to see that Mark's very brevity offers opportunities to unpack meaning and application to contemporary life—perhaps easier for someone who has experienced life and work outside the Christian bubble. And this gospel also affords chances to exercise one's imagination to fill out the picture it portrays.

This commentary will present the results of a close reading of Mark. I have used the New Revised Standard Version (NRSV) for the text as it is used currently in the Episcopal churches I attend.

Introduction

It presents my own thoughts upon a careful consideration of the text. In a few instances, I have done some rudimentary research to clarify my understanding of ancient geography, biblical references, and Judaic practices. I have applied such skills and mental habits as I have acquired from a career in law, a love of history, and an appreciation for great literature, especially short stories and poetry. I am also indebted to my wife and her family for deepening my knowledge of (and joy from) Judaism and Jewish culture. This led me to see how important and illuminating they are to what Mark describes.

I have tried to put myself in the place of someone in the first century who had this Gospel alone—Matthew, Luke, and John not having been written yet—to be introduced to Jesus and his followers. How would someone in their position react? What questions would they have? Christianity as a religion would be in its infancy. What does Mark, necessarily unencumbered with what the other gospels present and 2,000 years of teaching, preaching, interpretations, traditions, and debate, tell us about Jesus and his message?

I hope, gentle reader, that you will approach my commentary in that spirit and derive some benefit from it. Indeed, I will go further. If you are an unbeliever, a seeker of something in which to believe, or a former, now disenchanted believer, perhaps you especially can put yourself in the place of someone in the first century encountering this gospel. I would ask you to consider whether this gives you hope of something better and higher than the cynicism and brutishness of the twenty-first century.

1

The Headlines

In those days Jesus came from Nazareth of Galilee and was baptized by John in the Jordan. And just as he was coming up out of the water, he saw the heavens torn apart and the Spirit descending like a dove on him. And a voice came from heaven, "You are my Son, the Beloved; with you I am well pleased." And the Spirit immediately drove him out into the wilderness. He was in the wilderness forty days, tempted by Satan; and he was with the wild beasts; and the angels waited on him. Now after John was arrested, Jesus came to Galilee, proclaiming the good news of God, and saying, "The time is fulfilled, and the kingdom of God has come near; repent, and believe in the good news." (Mark 1:9–15)

IF THE GOSPEL OF Mark is the executive summary, chapter 1 contains the headlines. Verse 1 states plainly, "The beginning of the good news of Jesus Christ, the Son of God." Right off the bat, the author is direct: I'm going to tell you about Jesus, it's good news, and he is the Son of God. No suggestiveness, no allusion, no draw-your-own-conclusions, no incrementalism as we get into the story.

For all the bluntness, there is something literary and learned from the start. The first words echo Genesis—"In the beginning"—and thus position the story of Jesus, his good news, as a new beginning. The next two verses quote the Prophet Isaiah, rooting the

The Executive Summary

story and the author in Judaism. The quoted verses from Isaiah point to another recent and notable Jewish religious figure, John the baptizer. And those coming out to John for baptism and repentance were Jews—"the whole Judean countryside and all the people of Jerusalem." Jesus begins his ministry only after John was arrested, thus linking the two. Jumping slightly ahead, Jesus's first act after calling his first disciples, the two sets of brothers, Simon and Andrew and James and John, is to teach in the synagogue in Capernaum—not in the marketplace, not in a city square, not in the countryside, but in a religious gathering place of Jews on the Jewish Sabbath. Thus, the sub-headline to the main headline is that Jesus stands on a foundation of Judaism. He is not some Northern European who inexplicably winds up in ancient Israel offering something alien to Judaism.

Now for what journalists would call "the lede:" the first quoted words of Jesus in the oldest source we have of him. "The time is fulfilled, and the kingdom of God has come near; repent, and believe in the good news." The first we hear from him is packed with his key points:

- The time is fulfilled—we are reaching a juncture, a culmination. What we have been waiting and hoping for is arriving.
- The kingdom of God has come near (or "is at hand")—the destination at which we are arriving is a kingdom—not a republic, not a dictatorship, not some other ruling configuration with which mankind was familiar or which it might imagine, and not a state of nature. But in this kingdom, God is the king. Men and women are his subjects. The relationships between them are those that prevail in such a polity. (It is hard for us in the twenty-first century, inured to republics and democracies, to comprehend what must have been naturally sensed by those who were accustomed to what was implied by the term "kingdom.")
- Repent—the very first act required is acknowledgement of sins and contrition for them.

- Believe in the good news—belief, i.e, faith, is next, but the belief, the faith, is that something good will happen.

It is all there. One might even conclude that this is everything crucial that Jesus had to say. All of the rest of his teaching was an elaboration of these core points. The kingdom of God is within reach. Repent. Believe.

The message is urgent. Chapter 1 begins this theme, repeated throughout Mark's Gospel, by the use of the terms "immediately" and "at once," to take us to new developments in the account. The Spirit "immediately" drives him into the wilderness. When he comes into Galilee with his core message and sees the two sets of brothers, he "immediately" calls them, and they "immediately" follow him. The chapter says that his fame spread throughout Galilee "at once."

Something is missing from chapter 1 of Mark compared to the other gospels. It concerns the question: Where did Jesus come from? Mark offers no account of Jesus's birth, his lineage, or his childhood. Jesus's divinity comes not from a virgin birth but from the Spirit descending upon him after his baptism by John. A voice from heaven—it can only be God—says that "You are my Son." And so, Jesus is anointed; he becomes the Christ (from the ancient Greek, "the anointed one"). He was a man who emerged, and after the baptism of repentance was touched and adopted by God. Where he came from was either not of consequence to or taken for granted by the author of Mark. In any event, this is a foundation story different from those offered by Luke, Matthew, and John.

Other passages in chapter 1 raise more questions. The calling of Simon and Andrew and then James and John: Why these two sets of brothers? Why brothers? Why tradesmen? And why did they drop everything—they were busy with their work, fishing, after all—and follow Jesus? There is no indication that they knew who he was. Who among us, on our way to a meeting or otherwise engaged in making a living, would do that?

There follow three healing miracles: the man with the unclean spirit, Simon's mother-in-law in bed with a fever, and the leper.

The Executive Summary

The man in the synagogue with the unclean spirit: What is an unclean spirit? Was it some type of psychological malady, like schizophrenia? The congregation seemed to recognize an unclean spirit not only as some type of mental or physical condition, but also as a defilement—evil. In any event, Jesus's ability to command the unclean spirit and rid the man of it was evidence of his divine powers. The unclean spirit explicitly recognizes him as the "Holy One of God," and the congregants are astonished at his ability to deal with it.

The second healing miracle may admit of a humorous possibility. It occurs at the home of Simon and Andrew and involves Simon's mother-in-law. (Wait a minute—Simon, i.e., Peter, is married? Who's the lucky gal? We never hear anything about her.) His mother-in-law is in bed with a fever. It sounds like Jesus and his disciples—James and John are with him—were looking for something to eat. Instead, on arrival, they found a kvetchy mother-in-law who is "sick." Anyone familiar with Jewish mothers-in-law will be familiar with the phenomenon. Indeed, "mother-in-law" is an almost guaranteed laugh line in Jewish humor. (E.g., Henny Youngman: "Just got back from a pleasure trip. I took my mother-in-law to the airport.") All that Jesus does is "take her by the hand" and lift her up. That could be more like gentle persuasion from a guest she wasn't expecting, but is OK with, rather than a miraculous cure. One can imagine her saying, "All right, all right. I'll get you something to eat. You, I like." But (turning to Simon, her no-good son-in-law, and making a face) she says, "No thanks to you!" Then again, changing the mind of an obstinate mother-in-law may truly be miraculous. Does Mark have a sense of humor? Does Jesus? Does God? Why not?

In any event, the first two healings are done openly; Jesus makes no secret of them. And they lead "the whole city" to seek Jesus to cure others who were sick or possessed by demons. The healing of the leper seems to have been done privately, i.e., just between Jesus and the leper, since Jesus sends the leper away, "sternly warning him" to "say nothing to anyone." This is the first time that Jesus admonishes someone that what he has done is not to be bruited about. Why? One explanation may be that Jesus does not want to be known as just a healer. (I have heard some scholars say that healers were not unusual in pre-modern societies like ancient Israel.) He has bigger goals and does not want the healing stories to divert attention from them. Another possibility is psychological—one way to make sure that something becomes known is tell someone that it is a secret. And indeed, the cured leper "went out and began to proclaim it freely, and to spread the word." Perhaps Jesus cleverly *wanted* the word to get out to attract more to his message. But this is a bit cynical.

One additional important development in chapter 1 is that Jesus decides that it is time for him and the disciples to broaden his work. He has generated great interest in and around Capernaum. Now after praying, he says, "Let us go on to the neighboring towns, so that I may proclaim the message there also; for that is what I came out to do." And so, "he went throughout Galilee." Jesus and some Jewish guys are going on a road trip!

In chapter 1, Mark has grabbed our attention. The reader wants to know what comes next. But before finding out, the historian in me wants to pause to consider the issue of evidence. What is the basis for Mark's account? The author doesn't say. But a close reading suggests that at least three sources were used that his first readers were likely to recognize. First, there is what we might call direct evidence—quotations of what Jesus said, things that he and the disciples did. These were probably mostly heard, observed, and experienced by the disciples and passed down orally to followers in the early years after Jesus's ministry. Second, there is a form of indirect evidence. These would be things only Jesus would have experienced (e.g., his baptism, his time in the wilderness), but must have been subsequently related by him to the disciples. One could imagine Jesus telling one or more of them in conversations about these occurrences over a meal or as they were traveling. Third, there is extrinsic evidence—what was known beyond what Jesus and the disciples said and did. Sources would be Jewish scriptures (e.g., Isaiah) and the history of the period in which Jesus conducted his ministry (e.g., John the Baptist).

2

The Conflict Begins

When Jesus saw their faith, he said to the paralytic, "Son, your sins are forgiven." Now some of the scribes were sitting there, questioning in their hearts, "Why does this fellow speak in this way? It is blasphemy! Who can forgive sins but God alone?" At once Jesus perceived in his spirit that they were discussing these questions among themselves; and he said to them, "Why do you raise such questions in your hearts? Which is easier, to say to the paralytic, 'Your sins are forgiven,' or to say, 'Stand up and take your mat and walk'? But so that you may know that the Son of Man has authority on earth to forgive sins"—he said to the paralytic—"I say to you, stand up, take your mat and go to your home." And he stood up, and immediately took the mat and went out before all of them; so that they were all amazed and glorified God, saying, "We have never seen anything like this!" (Mark 2:5–12)

BEFORE TURNING TO THE heart of chapter 2, we have to note, if we are reading closely, something puzzling and interesting. It is probably owing to the "executive summary" nature of Mark. Verse 1 of chapter 2 begins by stating that Jesus "returned to Capernaum after some days" and that it was reported he was "at home." Not Nazareth, the place where chapter 1 told us he came from and where the unclean spirit stated that he was from? If he was living in Capernaum, how did he come to make it his home? What were his living arrangements like? The Gospel of Mark is not infrequently like this; it is easy to blow past unelaborated details in the author's compression of the story.

This aside, the main development in chapter 2 is the beginning of Jesus's conflict with the scribes and Pharisees. For the first time, Jesus and the disciples have run-ins with them. One happens when he heals the paralytic. Jesus tells him that his sins are forgiven, and the scribes object that this is blasphemy since only God can forgive sins. Jesus responds sharply, and asserts his authority to do so. They also criticize his dining with tax collectors and sinners. Jesus answers that his role is like a physician; sinners need such a doctor, not the righteous. In addition, the Pharisees question the failure of Jesus's disciples to fast, as the Pharisees do. In response, Jesus compares his disciples to wedding guests and himself to the bridegroom; fasting is thus inappropriate. Relatedly, the disciples work on the Sabbath—they pluck heads of grain as they go through a grainfield—which the Pharisees point out is not lawful. Jesus's retort is that the Sabbath was made for mankind and not the other way around and, in any event, he is the Lord of the Sabbath.

One can imagine, and the rest of the Gospel will show, that the Pharisees are unpersuaded and undeterred by Jesus's comebacks. But even so, this is a debate within, and not with, Judaism. As chapter 1 showed, Jesus is teaching and offering his message in synagogues. And when he healed the leper, Jesus told him to "show yourself to the priest, and offer for your cleansing what Moses commanded." This was not a rejection of Judaism and Jewish practice. Jesus may be offering something new—a new piece of cloth, new wine and fresh wineskins, to use his metaphors. But it is still Jewish clothing and Jewish wine. (Manischewitz, anyone?)

Perhaps that is how the term, "the Son of Man," can be best understood. Jesus uses it for the first time in chapter 2. After some cursory research, I gather that this term has been the subject of scholarly dispute. It has its origins in the Torah but only as a way of describing mankind in general. Jesus gives it a twist and seems to invest it with a more specific and bigger meaning as a title for himself. Yet it recalls his human nature, his emergence as a man anointed by God. Once again, a Jewish foundation, but something new added.

3

Unclean Spirits and True Kindred

> *He told his disciples to have a boat ready for him because of the crowd, so that they would not crush him; for he had cured many, so that all who had diseases pressed upon him to touch him. Whenever the unclean spirits saw him, they fell down before him and shouted, "You are the Son of God!" But he sternly ordered them not to make him known. . . . Then he went home; and the crowd came together again, so that they could not even eat. When his family heard it, they went out to restrain him, for people were saying, "He has gone out of his mind." . . . Then his mother and his brothers came; and standing outside, they sent to him and called him. A crowd was sitting around him; and they said to him, "Your mother and your brothers and sisters are outside, asking for you." And he replied, "Who are my mother and my brothers?" And looking at those who sat around him, he said, "Here are my mother and my brothers! Whoever does the will of God is my brother and sister and mother." (Mark 3:9–12, 19–21, 31–35)*

REINFORCING THAT WE ARE still operating within Judaism, chapter 3 begins, "Again he entered the synagogue." Mark doesn't explicitly say which synagogue, but the only one we have heard about that he could "again" enter was in Capernaum. There, Jesus performs another healing, this time of the man with the withered hand, and he does so on the Sabbath, which sets up more conflict with the scribes and Pharisees. Urgency continues as the Pharisees "immediately" conspire with a new set of players, "the Herodians," probably flunkies of King Herod, the Roman stooge, to destroy Jesus.

We may call chapter 3 the "unclean spirits" chapter. After departing for the sea, word gets around, and Jesus attracts big crowds from many regions, so large that they threaten to "crush" him. This is because he is curing many. Some of those he is curing evidently have unclean spirits because we are told they fall down before him and shout "You are the Son of God!" Once again, Jesus admonishes them "not to make him known." Why? It is one thing not to want to be pigeon-holed as a mere healer. It is another to try to keep quiet who he really is. Perhaps because it is premature in the unfolding of his ministry (and Mark's story)? It is also a bit puzzling to note that, so far, it is only the unclean spirits who have recognized him—here in chapter 3 and also in chapter 1. Again, why? If it is first the forces of evil, and Satan himself, who recognize the representative of God, and God himself, perhaps this tells us something about the reality and strength of evil and Satan?

Unclean spirits also provide the subject of a major debate between Jesus and the scribes. (More argument within Judaism.) They come down from Jerusalem to diagnose Jesus's problem—he has "Beelzebul," the ruler of demons, they say, and by Beelzebul "he casts out demons." Jesus has a riposte: "How can Satan cast out Satan?" He continues with the famous passage relied upon by Abraham Lincoln in his House Divided speech on slavery, and brings the argument on division back to Satan by observing that if Satan has risen up against himself, he cannot stand and is at an end. The scribes' argument, Jesus shows, ends in contradiction, a logical *tour de force* that Lincoln would have loved.

Jesus then makes two additional points: (1) no one can plunder the house of a "strong man" without first tying him up, and (2) a distinction about forgiveness of sins and blasphemies. On this latter point, Jesus says that sins and blasphemies can be forgiven in general, but that blasphemy against the Holy Spirit cannot be forgiven and is an eternal sin. The connection of these two points to the debate with the scribes is difficult to discern.

The second point may be explicable as an accusation against the scribes. By characterizing Jesus as possessed by Satan, Jesus may be saying that they have in fact blasphemed the Holy Spirit, an unforgivable sin, since it is by the Holy Spirit that he is acting when he casts out demons.

The first point, however, is harder to connect with what Jesus has previously stated. Since Mark says that Jesus was speaking in parables, who is the "strong man?" Is it Jesus himself? Can his "house," i.e., what he is trying to establish, only be plundered, i.e., defeated, if he is neutralized? But in the end, Jesus cannot be neutralized. He is the Son of God, as Mark told us at the outset. Is the strong man Satan? Is Jesus saying that the only way to save the souls of those afflicted by unclean spirits is effectively to tie up Satan by casting him out and then plundering the house that Satan tried to set up in those possessed? But our first reaction to hearing the teaching about the strong man is that he has been robbed and done an injustice. The good guy/bad guy roles seem reversed. And how does this fit with the insightful and understandable point about division failing? It seems a different metaphor.

Two other significant developments occur in chapter 3. When Jesus goes up the mountain, he calls the twelve apostles. All of them are named. (Interestingly, Levi, the tax collector, whom Jesus called in chapter 2, to the consternation of the scribes, is not named. Another son of Alphaeus, James, is. What happened to Levi?) Mark says that Jesus gives them three tasks: (1) to be with him; (2) to be sent out to proclaim the message; and (3) to cast out demons. A three-fold theme is now appearing. In chapter 1, it was three miracles of healing. In chapter 3, the apostles have three tasks. And all three persons of the Trinity have made their appearance—God, Son, and Holy Spirit.

Jesus is the Son of God, we understand from Mark. But he is also the Son of Man. We get additional insights in chapter 3 into Jesus as a man. In the first episode of chapter 3, the healing of the man with the withered hand, Jesus's reaction to the scribes'

The Executive Summary

disapproval is anger and grief. He can also be stern, as when he orders the demons that he has cast out not to make him known. Moreover, in the midst of his dispute with the scribes at his home, Jesus's family comes looking for him. We learn that they consist of his mother and multiple brothers and sisters. No father is mentioned. (We are not told where they live. Capernaum too? What happened to Nazareth?) They are there to restrain him because "people were saying, 'He has gone out of his mind.'" In other words, Jesus is also seen by some in the community as a religious kook (or worse), and his family feels that they must take him in hand.

Jesus's retort to the scribes is also a rebuke to his family. And he drives the point home when his mother and brothers call to him outside his home. (His only parent and brothers—the men in the family—are trying to "restrain him." One can imagine the looks on their faces and the tone of their voices—worry, pain, anger, disgust. This is not the Mary of Luke, and his brothers are by no means followers.) Jesus says that his followers—those who do the will of God—are his mother and brothers. It is an implicit rejection of his natural family and an adoption of a spiritual one. Jesus makes here a point beyond giving his natural family the back of his hand. It is that even something as apparently ineradicable as a flesh-and-blood family can be a matter of choice for an individual. We are not prisoners of fate. We are free to decide to follow (or not) our Father in heaven.

4

Teaching

When he was alone, those who were around him along with the twelve asked him about the parables. And he said to them, "To you has been given the secret of the kingdom of God, but for those outside, everything comes in parables; in order that
'they may indeed look, but not perceive,
and may indeed listen, but not understand;
so that they may not turn again and be forgiven.'"
. . . On that day, when evening had come, he said to them, "Let us go across to the other side." And leaving the crowd behind, they took him with them in the boat, just as he was. Other boats were with him. A great windstorm arose, and the waves beat into the boat, so that the boat was already being swamped. But he was in the stern, asleep on the cushion; and they woke him up and said to him, "Teacher, do you not care that we are perishing?" He woke up and rebuked the wind, and said to the sea, "Peace! Be still!" Then the wind ceased, and there was a dead calm. He said to them, "Why are you afraid? Have you still no faith?"
(Mark 4:10–12, 35–40)

IN CHAPTER 4, MARK shows Jesus diving into teaching. Indeed, we might call this the parables chapter since it recounts multiple teachings of this sort. Not that Jesus hasn't been teaching before; as in chapter 3, Mark begins chapter 4 by stating that "again"

The Executive Summary

Jesus does something, in this case "teach beside the sea." What is implied by the "again" usage? The term suggests repetition. Jesus is not about mere novelty. He came to do certain things—e.g., heal, teach—and was ready to repeat them to get his message across.

As Professor Garwood Anderson of Nashotah House pointed out in an online course I took on the parables, Jesus uses situations and figures of speech with which his listeners would have been familiar in the countryside and villages of ancient Israel. But the stories come with a twist—something different and even strange. All of the parables in chapter 4 are like this, and drive us sometimes to think in new ways.

The first is the parable of the sower. He spreads seed in several different places—on a path, on stony ground, in ground covered with thorns, and on good soil. The seed only takes lasting root in good soil and bears fruit. It fails for various reasons in the other places: the birds eat the seed on the path, the rocky soil lacks depth, the thorns choke growth. Later, with the twelve and "those who were around him"—who are they?—Jesus explains the meaning of the parable. The seed is "the word," and it fails because Satan takes away the word (the path), "trouble or persecution" cause those who at first readily received the word to fall away immediately (the rocky ground), the "cares of the world, the lure of wealth, and the desire for other things" choke the word (the thorns). At one level, this sounds pretty straightforward. If Jesus's auditors are good soil, all is well. So, be good soil, and avoid reasons the seed fails—the lure of wealth, desire for other things.

But some of the reasons are not so avoidable and may be out of one's control. If you are on the path, according to Jesus, "Satan immediately comes and takes away the word." Well, Satan is a pretty formidable foe, and he is the one who takes it away. Those on the path don't give it up. Similarly, for those on rocky ground, "trouble or persecution arises." They don't cause the trouble, and necessarily persecution makes them victims, not perpetrators. One could say that they should bear their troubles or persecution, but that is a stiff demand. Those among the thorns have a weaker case, but the cares of the world can be pretty tough. Even the lure of wealth and desire for other things are susceptible to some nuance. What if the ends of wealth and desire for things are good—e.g., providing for one's family, giving them opportunities for a better life? The parable also begs the question of how individuals found themselves in these different positions. If they put themselves there, that's one thing. But suppose they were born into, or had no choice but to be on, the path or on rocky soil or among thorns? The seed—God's grace—may be generously and lavishly spread as Rev. Luis Leon, retired Rector of St. John's, Lafayette Square, once preached. But only those on good soil thrive.

Several more parables are presented in Mark 4:21–32. There is some ambiguity about to whom Jesus is teaching with these parables since Mark says that he is speaking to "them." At first, we might suppose that it is only his disciples since Jesus has just finished explaining the meaning of the sower parable to them. But since Jesus says that those on the outside are taught only in parables, it would seem that the series that begin at verse 21 are for that larger audience.

In any event, the parables continue with the one on measures. The measure you give will be the measure you get, and still more will be given you. Once again, so far, so good—kind of expected, and reminiscent of the Beatles song, *The End*. But then the twist comes: "For to those who have, more will be given; and from those who have nothing, even what they have will be taken away." Ouch! That sounds cruel. Another older song comes to mind, *Ain't We Got Fun?* ("The rich get richer and the poor get . . . children").

The next two parables that Jesus offers explicitly concern the kingdom of God. Jesus frames them as metaphors for that kingdom. In one, we are back to farming—the spreading of seed. "Someone" does so, sleeps and rises night and day, and yet "does not know how" the seed sprouts and grows. When the grain is ripe, he "goes in with his sickle" to harvest it. Presumably the farmer is the Father—God. However, here comes the twist again. He doesn't know how the grain grows. Is God less than all-knowing? And when there is a good outcome, ripe grain, he cuts it down. And if we are the grain in the parable, is the kingdom violent? The harvest is good—for God. What happens to the grain? Like the measure parable, the grain harvest parable has a disturbing quality.

This is followed by a parable that Jesus begins by asking rhetorically "With what can we compare the kingdom of God, or what parable will we use for it?" At this point, in that society and clime, one can imagine that his listeners were ready, as New Testament scholar John Dominic Crossan once suggested on a PBS show about Jesus, for a description of paradise—flowing waters, trees bearing abundant fruit and providing shade from the hot sun, perhaps even lovely maidens. Instead, Jesus says that it is like a mustard seed! The entire parable is a twist. True, he tries to make it sound good; the small mustard seed grows into "the greatest of all shrubs," and birds nest in it. But it's still just a shrub, not the towering cedars of Lebanon or some other magnificent tree.

How are the parables of chapter 4 tied together? At a metaphoric level, they all involve seed. (Even the measure parable can, since in ancient Israel's agrarian economy measures must have contained seed and its products.) God creates the seed and sows it. It grows, or not. It is tiny, but has the potential to become something good and great. We are that seed with that potential. At a cosmic level, all the parables are Jesus's attempts at describing the kingdom of God. He says so explicitly in two of them. And when Jesus explains the sower parable to the twelve and the others around him, he says that "[t]o you has been given the secret of the kingdom of God." Recall Jesus's first quoted words in Mark: "The time is fulfilled, and the kingdom of God has come near." In chapter 4, Mark is telling us what Jesus taught to give meaning to those headlines.

There is still one more troubling aspect, however, to what Jesus says in chapter 4. He speaks to the masses—the ordinary people—in parables. But he explains their meaning to his disciples secretly. Mark mentions this secrecy several times in chapter 4. Why would Jesus do that? Why does he set up a dichotomy between the *hoi polloi* and the insiders? One possibility is that looking ahead to the culmination of his ministry, Jesus is preparing a select group he has called to carry on what he has taught. Not that they are better, he just wants to make sure they understand.

They are to be "the lamp" that is not "to be put under the bushel basket." And Mark lets us know that the secrets can't be kept, as he has Jesus say "For there is nothing hidden, except to be disclosed; nor is anything secret, except to come to light." And to make sure, Mark, slyly, has revealed them.

As for the rest of us, we are taught, but in a way where we must draw our own conclusions, believe or not, and act accordingly. It is up to us. As Jesus says, "Let anyone with ears to hear listen!" God sows our seed, but He does not know how or even whether we will grow. We may ultimately "indeed look, but not perceive, and may indeed listen, but not understand." If so, we "may not turn again and be forgiven." But if we do understand rightly, believe, and act as God hopes and wishes, we will bear fruit many times over, be part of a good harvest, be great, and for all our faults, be forgiven. The parables can seem jarring and unfair by human standards. But not by kingdom standards. Jesus is giving a description of the kingdom of God, a new vision of reality. He is provoking us to think how we get there.

To underscore that the disciples are not on a better footing than the rest of us, Mark offers us the account of the boat trip to end chapter 4. Jesus says that they should go to "the other side." "They"—it's clear that Mark is talking about the disciples here—took Jesus "just as he was." (What does this mean?) A great windstorm arises, and the boat threatens to go down. And Jesus is asleep in the stern! The disciples are terrified and wake him up. He rebukes the wind and sea, and calm returns. (Perhaps the storm reflects the disciples' own consternation at Jesus's teachings as they are trying to reach "the other side"—understanding and eternal life.) And here the point is made: Jesus rebukes the disciples too, saying: "Why are you afraid? Have you still no faith?" Jesus links fear and faith, and states that faith can overcome fear. As he said at the outset, "believe in the good news." The story of the windstorm begins to tease out the meaning of this. We may also recall another biblical consideration of fear in the Psalms, where we are told that fear of God is the beginning of wisdom. And so, chapter 4 ends with Jesus giving us another twist.

5

Healing

They came to the other side of the sea, to the country of the Gerasenes. And when he had stepped out of the boat, immediately a man out of the tombs with an unclean spirit met him. He lived among the tombs; and no one could restrain him any more, even with a chain; for he had often been restrained with shackles and chains, but the chains he wrenched apart, and the shackles he broke in pieces; and no one had the strength to subdue him. Night and day among the tombs and on the mountains he was always howling and bruising himself with stones. When he saw Jesus from a distance, he ran and bowed down before him; and he shouted at the top of his voice, "What have you to do with me, Jesus, Son of the Most High God? I adjure you by God, do not torment me." For he had said to him, "Come out of the man, you unclean spirit!" . . . When Jesus had crossed again in the boat to the other side, a great crowd gathered around him; and he was by the sea. Then one of the leaders of the synagogue named Jairus came and, when he saw him, fell at his feet and begged him repeatedly, "My little daughter is at the point of death. Come and lay your hands on her, so that she may be made well, and live." So he went with him. . . . He took her by the hand and said to her, "Talitha cum," which means, "Little girl, get up!" And immediately the girl got up and began to walk about (she was twelve years of age). At this they were overcome with amazement. He strictly ordered them

Healing

that no one should know this, and told them to give her something to eat. (Mark 5:1–8, 21–24, 41–43)

IN CHAPTER 5, JESUS returns to healing. In recounting three new instances (another three-fold set), Mark has Jesus show us more about what he is healing, who can be healed, and how healing can happen. We also learn more about how he is going to pursue his mission, and the case is built for his identity as the Son of God.

The first healing episode in chapter 5 is the episode of the Gerasene (sometimes called Gadarene) swine. Jesus is now in "the country of the Gerasenes." A bit of research reveals that this is territory on the eastern side of the Sea of Galilee. A league of cities called the Decapolis is there, including Gerasa and Gedara. These are Greco-Roman cities in population and culture. They are outposts of the Gentile world.

When Jesus lands after his trip across the sea, immediately—there it is again—a man from the tombs with an unclean spirit meets him. Jesus tells the unclean spirit to come out of the man, and after a fascinating exchange, the unclean spirits—it turns out there are many of them—are sent into a herd of swine which rush down a bank into the sea and are drowned.

How we get to this result is revealing, but also, as usual, question-provoking. Once again, it is unclean spirits who recognize Jesus for who he is. The possessed man shouts "What have you to do with me, Jesus, Son of the Most High God?" We get insights into the nature of unclean spirits. They are strong; they allow the man to wrench apart chains and break shackles. Mark reports that "No one had the strength to subdue him." They also cause the man to be self-destructive. He continually is howling and "bruising himself with stones." They are associated with death. The man lives among tombs, and when they are cast out of the man and enter the swine, they are drowned. And we learn their name—"Legion," as there are many of them. They know that they are unclean. When they and Jesus confront each other, they ask to be sent into the swine—unclean animals whose meat is prohibited by Jewish dietary laws. That is where they know they belong. The attributes that we learn about the unclean spirits tell us about the devil and his accomplices.

The unclean spirits recognize Jesus's greater power. They beg him, and he commands them. But here the questions start. Why do they ask Jesus "not to send them out of the country?" What is the import of that? Why is being sent into swine better? Even though Jesus has power over them, Mark tells us that "he gave them permission" to enter the swine. This is an odd formulation. Why doesn't Jesus exercise his power and just cast them into the herd?

The aftermath of the episode is suggestive. Of course, the swineherds, watching stupefied, run off and tell about it in the city and country. People come to see what has happened, and they find the demoniac, calmly sitting there, clothed, and in his right mind. What is their reaction—joy, gratitude, admiration? No!—"they were afraid." And they beg Jesus too—"to leave their neighborhood." And Jesus doesn't preach to them or remonstrate. He complies and gets back in the boat that brought him. His parting shot, however, is to the former demoniac, who also begs. In his case, however, the begging is to go with Jesus. Jesus declines. Instead, Jesus tells the man to tell all his friends about the mercy the Lord has shown him. Mark reports that he did so, proclaiming his story in the Decapolis—it is named as such in Mark.

More questions: Why were the people afraid? And even more to the point, why didn't Jesus admonish them for their fear and adjure their faith as he does others? Why doesn't Jesus let the demoniac come with him? He sounds like a more than willing follower with a proof point to make. Why did Jesus *not* tell the demoniac to tell no one, as he had told others after healing miracles, and in fact to do the opposite? Why does Jesus leave so soon and after running into a little skepticism?

Perhaps we can discern some answers by recalling where Jesus was—Gentile territory. Indeed, it may be a fair inference that the demoniac was a Gentile. The good news is that Jesus is prepared to take his message to the Gentiles and heal them too. Since they *are* Gentiles and not Jews who should know better, he is willing to excuse their fear. And he will not push things too far with them. If they want him to leave, he will. But he does want the message to start to get out among them, and so he tells the former demoniac to remain, tell what happened, and make it clear that it was through the Lord's mercy—not the machinations of pagan deities. The story of the Gerasene swine thus tells us that Jesus's mission is fundamentally a Jewish operation but open to others.

Back goes Jesus across the sea to more familiar ground and to more healing. One instance is intentional, the other is inadvertent. In the first case, Jairus, one of the leaders of the synagogue (the exact place is not identified), has a twelve-year-old daughter who is close to dying. (Synagogues remain part of Jesus's life; he does not simply leave them behind as he did the country of the Gerasenes.) The synagogue leader "begged" Jesus repeatedly—there is that word again—to make her well. As Jesus is pushing through a crowd to go to the girl, a woman who has been suffering from hemorrhages for twelve years touches Jesus's cloak from behind. This stops her bleeding, and she feels herself become well. "Immediately"—here we go again—Jesus realizes that "power had gone forth from him." He asks, "Who touched my clothes?" At this point, I once again imagine a humorous and very Jewish exchange taking place. The disciples reply by pointing out the crowd pressing in on Jesus and ask, "how can you say 'Who touched me?'" This sounds like familiar Jewish humor where one question is answered sarcastically with another question that makes the first question sound pretty dumb. Basically, the disciples are saying, "How should we know? You haven't noticed the crowd?"

More seriously, and back to the story, the woman falls down before Jesus and fesses up. She comes "in fear and trembling." Jesus reassures her that her "faith has made you well." The connection between fear and faith is thus again made. Faith is the key. Believe in the good news.

By this point, people inform Jesus and Jairus that his daughter is dead. Has the inadvertent healing of the woman tragically diverted Jesus from saving the girl? Jesus's response echoes what he has just told the woman: "Do not fear, only believe." Fear or faith?

The Executive Summary

Part of Jesus's core message is to have faith. And over the derision of the crowd, he cures the girl, who "immediately" gets up and walks about. Jesus has done this one privately, with only the parents and, intriguingly, Peter, James, and John, present. This is the first time that he separates those three from the other disciples; there will be other times. Why? And on this occasion, unlike across the sea, he "strictly ordered" that no one should be told about the healing. He has bigger things to do among his people. This episode ends with another Jewish moment that brings a smile. After the girl arises, Jesus tells her parents to give her something to eat, the reflexive Jewish offer upon any new arrival or development, much like the Episcopalian offer of a drink.

I have noted all the begging in chapter 5. There could have been other ways to describe the interactions between Jesus and those in chapter 5. They could have simply asked, or urged, or presumptuously directed. Instead, they beg. Someone who does so is acknowledging a superior—in authority, status, power, attainment, and so forth. And so, Jesus's stature is reinforced in chapter 5 by these descriptions. A variety of persons—not just unclean spirits—in a variety of situations intuitively are recognizing him as exalted—steps toward confirming the assertion with which Mark began—the good news of Jesus Christ, the Son of God.

One last note about the healing back home, as it were—both are females, one a girl, the other an adult woman. Both are daughters—the girl of Jairus, and the woman Jesus addresses as such. This implies that Jesus is in the role of a father to her and points also to something about his nature—the representative of the Father in heaven, the Son. And what to make of twelve years—the girl's age and the duration of the woman's hemorrhages, which parallel each other? Without going too far into mystical numerology, the number twelve has many references in the Bible: the twelve tribes of Israel, the twelve apostles, etc. There is a suggestion of importance and dignity in these females by the use of the number. Given the subordinate role of women in the society of Jesus's time, is he telling us something about the wide availability of God's healing grace?

6

Reprise

He called the twelve and began to send them out two by two, and gave them authority over unclean spirits . . . The apostles gathered around Jesus, and told him all that they had done and taught. He said to them, "Come away to a deserted place all by yourselves and rest a while." For many were coming and going, and they had no leisure even to eat. And they went away in the boat to a deserted place by themselves. Now many saw them going and recognized them, and they hurried there on foot from all the towns and arrived ahead of them. As he went ashore, he saw a great crowd; and he had compassion for them, because they were like sheep without a shepherd; and he began to teach them many things. When it grew late, his disciples came to him and said, "This is a deserted place, and the hour is now very late; send them away so that they may go into the surrounding country and villages and buy something for themselves to eat." But he answered them, "You give them something to eat." They said to him, "Are we to go and buy two hundred denarii worth of bread, and give it to them to eat?" And he said to them, "How many loaves have you? Go and see." (Mark 6:7, 30–38)

CHAPTER 6 REPRISES A number of features of Mark's Gospel thus far. Jesus is back in his "hometown" (Capernaum? Nazareth?) and teaching in the synagogue there. He gets a skeptical reaction again, as he did in chapter 3 and perhaps chapter 1. His family

The Executive Summary

background, evidently modest and unexceptional, figures into this reaction. Chapter 6 also gives us more on the relationship between Jesus and John the baptizer. In an extended interlude, Mark describes the infamous circumstances of John's execution by King Herod. It includes Herod's reaction to Jesus's growing notoriety—Herod believes John has been raised from the dead after Herod had him beheaded—and thus there is a foreshadowing of Jesus's resurrection. Mark also offers a moment of psychological insight about some powerful men: Even though John is undoubtedly critical of Herod and this "greatly perplexed" Herod, "yet he liked to listen to him." Those in power, to whom truth is spoken, can have a strange fascination for it.

In addition, we have another instance of Jesus retiring by himself to pray, as he did in chapter 1. That occasion led to his expansion of mission. Chapter 6 does not say what this period of prayer is going to lead to, but we now have an expectation that something bigger is going to happen. Chapter 6 has another storm besetting his disciples on the sea and Jesus calming the waters to their amazement, as occurred in chapter 4. And finally, there is more begging for healing and touching of his cloak that accomplishes it, as in chapter 5.

Thus, we may call chapter 6 the reprise chapter. This invites the question: why? Has Mark run out of things to tell us? I think that is too simple. If Mark's Gospel is an elaboration of the headlines announced by Jesus's first quoted words in chapter 1, Mark has no reservation about repetition, as I argued above. These similar incidents and developments deepen our understanding of the key points of Jesus's ministry and offer more information about him.

We learn more about Jesus's reactions. He was "amazed" at the unbelief of those in the synagogue. He has a wise perspective about it that he uses to counsel the twelve. He has understanding for their physical and psychological needs after they return from their journeys, flying solo, as it were, for the first time. He has compassion for the crowd that gathers for his teaching. He reassures the twelve when they are afraid.

Reprise

We also learn more details about his personal and family situation prior to the beginning of his ministry. The skeptics in the synagogue, while impressed by what he has to say and what he has done, "took offense" because he was just "the carpenter" and the son of Mary and the brother of James, Joses, Judas, and Simon, and various unnamed sisters. We thus have his mother and brothers identified (they were only generally described in chapter 3). Once again, there is no mention of a father, and nothing about a virgin birth or anything especially indicative in his childhood. Indeed, the whole point in Mark seems to be that Jesus emerged from nothing exceptional.

Chapter 6 does have two significant new developments. In both, he greatly expands the reach and impact of what he is trying to achieve. To use a modern baseball metaphor, Jesus moves from playing small ball, one base and one run at a time, and starts to play for three-run homers and the big inning.

First, Jesus delegates authority to the twelve. Up to this point, they have been recipients of his teaching—special recipients, to be sure, as his explanation of the parables to them shows—but just recipients as the crowds flocking to Jesus were, and just witnesses to his healing. Now, Jesus sends them out "two by two" and gives them authority over the unclean spirits that heretofore only Jesus possessed. And they are successful! One can imagine the excitement on their return as "[t]he apostles gathered around Jesus and told him all that they had done and taught." What an adrenaline rush! And twelve Jewish guys talking all at once! No wonder Jesus wisely tells them to come away to a deserted place and rest a while. But the big news here is that Jesus transfers his power to trusted agents and thereby multiplies the potential impact of his mission.

Second, we have the miracle of the loaves and fishes. This is also something new qualitatively and quantitatively. It is different from casting out unclean spirits, healing, or teaching. (By the way, in chapter 6, as in other places, Mark speaks generally of Jesus teaching, but does not provide specifics. Oh to have the content of that teaching along with the parables!) With the loaves and fishes, Jesus is literally nourishing. Moreover, he feeds a multitude—5,000

The Executive Summary

men. (He does so in the face of more quintessentially Jewish sarcasm from the disciples: "Are we to go and buy two hundred denarii worth of bread, and give it to them to eat?" That's months of wages; the disciples are saying, "what are we, made of money?") I do not doubt Jesus's ability to multiply the bread and fish to feed so many. As the Christ—the anointed one of God—he could do things beyond our extremely limited understanding of the physical universe. (And yet, in the face of the skepticism in his hometown synagogue, "he could do no deed of power there." Could unbelief be so powerful?) But Mark hints at a symbolic level of understanding the episode of the loaves and fishes.

After the loaves and fishes miracle, Jesus sends the disciples off to Bethsaida by boat and goes up the mountain to pray. As in chapter 4, the disciples run into trouble on the sea. And so, Jesus comes to them, walking on the sea and telling them not to be afraid. He gets in the boat and the wind ceases. Mark reports that the disciples are "utterly astounded"—understandably so. But then, seemingly elliptically, Mark links their reaction to the loaves: "for they did not understand about the loaves, but their hearts were hardened." How is their failure to understand the loaves related to being saved again at sea? Perhaps the explanation is that for all of their success on their first solo missions, the disciples still fail to see who Jesus is and what he is about. Like their consternation before on a troubled sea, they don't get it and remain afraid. Jesus has come to "feed" many spiritually if their hearts are not hardened—if they have faith. The 5,000 did and were fed. The disciples aren't quite there yet.

And of course, the urgency continues in Chapter 6—more instances of "immediately" and "at once." After the loaves and fishes, Jesus "immediately" makes the disciples board the boat to Bethsaida. When they are terrified on the sea, he "immediately" tells them "Take heart, it is I; do not be afraid." When they land at Gennesaret (not Bethsaida? Maybe they were blown off course), "at once" people recognize him and "rush" to bring the sick to him for healing. I read an exposition on the short story not long ago by George Saunders, *A Swim in the Pond in the Rain*. He examines the techniques of the great Russian writers—Turgenev, Chekhov, Tolstoy, Gogol. One of Saunders's key points is that a good short story is a system for the transfer of energy. Without in any way suggesting that Mark's Gospel is a work of fiction, I begin to see that Mark knew well the principles of how to advance a story.

7

Gentiles

Then he called the crowd again and said to them, "Listen to me, all of you, and understand: there is nothing outside a person that by going in can defile, but the things that come out are what defile.".. For it is from within, from the human heart, that evil intentions come: fornication, theft, murder, adultery, avarice, wickedness, deceit, licentiousness, envy, slander, pride, folly. All these evil things come from within, and they defile a person." From there he set out and went away to the region of Tyre. He entered a house and did not want anyone to know he was there. Yet he could not escape notice, but a woman whose little daughter had an unclean spirit immediately heard about him, and she came and bowed down at his feet. Now the woman was a Gentile, of Syrophoenician origin. She begged him to cast the demon out of her daughter. He said to her, "Let the children be fed first, for it is not fair to take the children's food and throw it to the dogs." But she answered him, "Sir, even the dogs under the table eat the children's crumbs." Then he said to her, "For saying that, you may go—the demon has left your daughter." So she went home, found the child lying on the bed, and the demon gone. (Mark 7:14–16, 21–30)

LIKE PREVIOUS CHAPTERS, CHAPTER 7 has a theme. It is the Gentile chapter or, more precisely, the chapter on relationships between

Gentiles and Jews. The entire chapter addresses this subject in one way or another.

The chapter begins with another cut-and-thrust between Jesus and the Pharisees and scribes. The latter have come from Jerusalem to—where? Chapter 6 left Jesus in Gennasaret, but chapter 7 does not specify where he is. In any event, the Pharisees criticize Jesus's disciples for eating with defiled hands and not honoring Jewish traditions.

Before providing Jesus's retort, Mark offers a short parenthetical primer on Jewish customs concerning cleanliness and the consumption of food. The manner and tone in which he does so suggests that the author is writing here with a non-Jewish audience in mind. He feels the need to explain what "the Jews" do and the traditions that "they" observe. With these comments, the author seems to be distancing himself from Jews. It almost invites the speculation that the author of Mark was himself not a Jew. It should be noted too that this digression is in contrast to Mark's presentation in earlier chapters of other ways that, according to the Pharisees and scribes, Jesus and his disciples flout Jewish traditions and customs. There, Mark simply states what Jesus and the disciples have done, the Pharisees' criticisms, and Jesus's rejoinders; it is assumed that the readers (other Jews?) will understand what the disputes are all about.

Putting these uncertainties aside, we see that Jesus's response to the Pharisees again anchors him in Judaism. He shows his deep knowledge of Hebrew Scriptures by utilizing Isaiah to criticize the Pharisees as hypocrites. And he further turns the tables on them by accusing them of exalting tradition—which Jesus knows well with his citation of Corban—over the commandments of God as presented by Moses. The argument between Jesus and the Pharisees and scribes thus remains a dispute within Judaism.

Or so it seems. Jesus then supplies another twist to what appears to be familiar ground. He calls to the crowd that has been apparently watching this verbal duel over Jewish practices, and says to them, "there is nothing outside a person that by going in can defile, but the things that come out are what defile." Later, when he is just with his disciples in "the house"—which house? where?—he elaborates. (They have come at least to understand Jesus's teaching methods, if not his message, by treating his pronouncement as a parable and asking for its meaning.) What matters, Jesus says, is the human heart and what comes from it. Evil actions arising from evil within—he provides a list—are what defile.

The connection of this to the Gentiles comes from the converse that Jesus also presents. He dismisses violations of the dietary restrictions—what comes from the outside—as not defiling since they concern the stomach and not the heart and ultimately wind up in the sewer. Mark adds another parenthetical that "[t]hus, he declared all foods clean." So, Gentiles can rest easy: Bacon and cheesesteaks are back on the menu! More seriously, Mark is here clarifying that, while Jesus's message is rooted in Judaism, Jewish tradition is not a barrier to non-Jews accepting Jesus. The teaching on defilement is for both Jews and Gentiles. What is in the heart is what matters.

Chapter 7 then takes us to two more stops on Jesus's itinerary. First, he sets out to the region of Tyre. This is intriguing. No mention is made of the disciples accompanying him. Did Jesus go alone? Mark says that he entered a house and did not want anyone to know he was there. Did Jesus, the man, need a break—some R&R? The destination is also suggestive. Tyre was a very ancient, non-Jewish city. It was a place that Jews historically considered evil, and the Hebrew prophets Ezekial and Isaiah foretold its destruction. Jesus thus ventures into not just Gentile territory, but particularly bad Gentile territory according to Jewish tradition. Isaiah, however, also foresaw Tyre rising again and accepting God. By placing Jesus in such a location, Mark thereby offers a Gentile parallel prefiguring Jesus's own destruction, rising from the dead, and acceptance as God, and subtly suggests that Gentiles may, and should, so recognize him.

But there is no rest for the weary in greater Tyre. Jesus "could not escape notice." A woman—Mark explicitly states that she was a Gentile—begs him—there it is again—to cast an unclean spirit—another one—out of her daughter. Jesus at first rebuffs her: "Let the children be fed first, for it is not fair to take the children's food and throw it to the dogs."

Ugh. It is not hard to understand Jesus as saying, the Jews come first, I'm here to take care of them, and the rest, like you, are dogs. That's pretty ugly. The best we can say is that maybe he was upset at having his vacation interrupted and, I suppose, he was making clear his Jewishness. But the Gentile woman understood a parable when she heard one, and turned the tables on *him* with her comment that even the dogs get to eat the children's crumbs. Touché! Jesus relents and heals her daughter. The twist to this story—a parable itself—is that Gentile faith can bring healing to Gentiles. Phew!

The next stop for Jesus is by way of Sidon—like Tyre, non-Jewish territory and synonymous with wickedness—and back to the region of the Decapolis—and still more Gentiles. (Mark has his geography mixed up since Sidon is north of Tyre and not on the way to the Decapolis.) Unlike his visit there recounted in chapter 5, things go differently for Jesus now. The people bring him a deaf man with a speech impediment and beg Jesus (more begging) to heal him. Jesus does so; "immediately" the man is cured. But this time, in contrast to his instructions to the demoniac but like those he gives in his Jewish homeland, Jesus orders them to tell no one. Of course, they ignore him and zealously proclaim what happened. And their reaction is different too. Instead of being afraid and begging Jesus to leave, they are astounded and praise him. Maybe the seeds planted in chapter 5 are starting to sprout. Regardless, Jesus has offered his message to Gentiles in multiple ways. They are part of his mission now as well. And by including them, Jesus engages in more force multiplication.

8

The Big Reveal

Jesus went on with his disciples to the villages of Caesarea Philippi; and on the way he asked his disciples, "Who do people say that I am?" And they answered him, "John the Baptist; and others, Elijah; and still others, one of the prophets." He asked them, "But who do you say that I am?" Peter answered him, "You are the Messiah." And he sternly ordered them not to tell anyone about him. (Mark 8:27–30)

CHAPTER 8 GIVES US a bit of everything—again, Mark has no hesitancy about repetition—and then offers the big reveal—Jesus's identity as the Messiah, his coming execution, and resurrection. We are only halfway through Mark's Gospel.

It is unclear where Jesus is as chapter 8 begins. His disciples are back with him. A "great crowd"—4,000 people—has assembled and been with him for three days. They are "in the desert." Since chapter 7 ended with Jesus in the region of the Decapolis, we might infer that he is still there, not in one of the cities but in the countryside somewhere. If this inference is correct, the great crowd may consist mostly of Gentiles. We are told that they have come "a great distance," perhaps from some of the ten Greco-Roman cities.

Another episode follows of feeding a multitude in an unlikely place with loaves and fishes. Why a repetition of this miracle? If Jesus is in Gentile territory and the crowd consists mostly of Gentiles,

Mark may be telling us that Jesus nourishes them as well as Jews. This would be consistent with the expansion of his mission that we saw in chapter 7. Jumping slightly ahead, on another boat trip, Jesus upbraids his disciples again for their failure to understand the latest loaves and fishes miracle, just as he had after the first one. He says, "Do you still not perceive or understand? Are your hearts hardened?" Recall that Mark suggested a symbolic level to the previous feeding miracle. That too is being reprised. The last time, it was a storm at sea that suggested the disciples' consternation. This time, however, it is because they don't have enough to eat on the trip. ("Now the disciples had forgotten to bring any bread; and they had only one loaf with them in the boat.") I have to observe another indication of Jewish humor. What is the equivalent to a storm at sea to a group of Jewish men? Not having enough to nosh on a trip! I surmise again that Mark and Jesus have a sense of humor even as they make an important point.

Jesus and the disciples are on the move in the rest of chapter 8, and their pace seems to be quickening. After feeding the great crowd, "immediately" Jesus and the disciples sail and go to "the district of Dalmanutha." This location too is uncertain, but recent archaeological work may have identified it on the western side of the Sea of Galilee. There, Jesus has another confrontation with the Pharisees who ask him for "a sign from heaven, to test him." This causes Jesus to "sigh deeply in his spirit" and then he says something a little puzzling: "Truly I tell you, no sign will be given to this generation." But what is the resurrection if not a sign? And Jesus is about to reveal it at the end of chapter 8. Jumping ahead, in chapter 13, he speaks extensively about signs. So, why does he state that no sign will be given to this generation?

In any event, Jesus and the disciples get back into the boat to go "across to the other side." This is when the exchange about the loaves and fishes with the disciples occurs. And then they come to Bethsaida where some people bring a blind man and "begged" Jesus to touch him. Jesus takes the man out of the village, cures him, and sends him home with yet another direction that he keep it to himself ("Do not even go into the village"). But like the latest

The Executive Summary

incident with the Pharisees, this healing has something a little odd. Jesus has one go at it, asks the man if he can see, and hears from him that the cure is only partial. Jesus has another go, and this one fully works. Why the double-clutch? Others were healed by simply touching his cloak unbeknownst to him. Here, he tries and doesn't fully succeed at first and has to try again. Why? As happened at the synagogue in his hometown and in the face of local skeptics, Jesus experiences a limit to his power.

Then it's on the road again, to the "villages of Caesarea Philippi." This is as far north as Tyre but well inland. On the way, we get the first revelation about who Jesus really is and what this really is all about. He asks the disciples who people say that he is. After they relate a few important prophetic figures in Judaism, Jesus asks the momentous question: "But who do you say that I am?" And Peter answers: "You are the Messiah."

So, it looks like the disciples' hearts are not completely hardened. With Peter's answer, the disciples, and we, begin to cross a Rubicon, as it were. But Jesus "sternly ordered" the disciples not to tell anyone about him just as he had admonished the unclean spirits who recognized him earlier. I can only infer that Jesus has more to do and that the time is not yet ripe for the disciples to be noising this about. Jesus then teaches the disciples about his forthcoming suffering, rejection by Jewish religious authorities, death, and rising after three days. He does this all "quite openly"—the big reveal—to the disciples and to us. That sounds to me, at the very least, like "a sign" is coming to this generation.

However, the disciples' hearts are not fully open since Peter is indignant about Jesus's predicted fate and, amazingly, "began to rebuke" Jesus. Not to put too fine a point on it, that takes some *chutzpah*! Jesus consequently rebukes Peter—"Get behind me Satan!"—and draws a distinction between focusing on divine things and human things.

Evidently there is a crowd nearby since Jesus calls to them at this point and offers a short sermon. The stakes, Jesus says, are huge, and what his followers must do is very demanding. They must do nothing less than reject the dictates and blandishments of the world, risk their very lives, and embrace him and the gospel he is preaching. It is a matter of ultimate life and death. And for the first time, in Jesus's speech, the cross as a symbol for followers makes its appearance. The Son of Man's suffering and death at the hands of the world and then his triumph over it is to be a model for the disciples and indeed for all his followers.

Some thoughts about why Jesus, and Mark, have chosen at this point to reveal all this: By now, Jesus knows that it will take some time and repetition for the disciples to grasp what he is saying. He has laid a foundation for them with his healing and teaching. But they struggle with it. The death and resurrection of the Messiah will be even harder for them, as Peter's reaction shows. Better to start now to prepare them. And us. The author of Mark knows that, like the disciples, we struggle with Jesus's message, what he has done, and what his resurrection means. The disciples' difficulties mirror our own and, in a way, encourage us. And so, better for the reader to start trying to wrap his head around all this, with more of the story yet to unfold.

9

Getting Ready

Six days later, Jesus took with him Peter and James and John, and led them up a high mountain apart, by themselves. And he was transfigured before them, and his clothes became dazzling white, such as no one on earth could bleach them. And there appeared to them Elijah with Moses, who were talking with Jesus. Then Peter said to Jesus, "Rabbi, it is good for us to be here; let us make three dwellings, one for you, one for Moses, and one for Elijah." He did not know what to say, for they were terrified. Then a cloud overshadowed them, and from the cloud there came a voice, "This is my Son, the Beloved; listen to him!" Suddenly when they looked around, they saw no one with them any more, but only Jesus. (Mark 9:2–8)

CHAPTER 9 FINISHES JESUS'S short sermon of chapter 8. It concludes with a contradiction of Jesus's reaction in chapter 8 to the Pharisees' demand for a sign. He says here that "[t]ruly I tell you, there are some standing here who will not taste death until they see that the kingdom of God has come with power." That's even more than a sign; it's the culmination. And it is consistent with Jesus's first words quoted in Mark—the kingdom of God is at hand. Be that as it may, chapter 9 principally tells of Jesus starting in earnest to prepare his disciples for what is to come. The sermon that ends chapter 8 and begins chapter 9 is part of this effort. Recall that it grew out of Jesus's colloquy with Peter about Jesus's identity and fate.

Chapter 9 also takes us up a high mountain with Peter, James, and John and to the encounter between Jesus and Elijah and Moses. Then, after a healing interlude with another unclean spirit, Jesus and the disciples travel through Galilee back to Capernaum. There, Jesus engages with the disciples at length, all of it with a view toward schooling the disciples for the future. This summary, however, glosses over a number of points that are curious, difficult and, frankly, elliptical at times.

Let's begin with the trip up the mountain. For some reason, Mark dates it with some specificity—"six days" after the sermon of late chapter 8/early chapter 9. But since we do not have a date for the sermon itself (or indeed anything in Mark's Gospel), we are left to wonder why the author felt a need to date the trip so exactly to six days later. As in chapter 5, Jesus pulls Peter, James, and John out of the twelve for the mountain trip. Why this inner-inner circle? In any event, Jesus is then transfigured, and Elijah and Moses appear and talk to Jesus. He is thus rooted again in Judaism; Elijah and Moses are two of the most important figures in Jewish history. Jesus is presented as on a par with them. But only briefly. They disappear and God's voice from heaven utters the same proclamation heard in chapter 1 as Jesus emerged from his baptism, but with the addition of "listen to him!" So, once again, we have something familiar and a twist. The biblical pattern of parallelism and expansion recurs. In the midst of all this, Peter and the others are understandably non-plussed—"terrified" actually. Peter babbles something about building three dwellings. Undoubtedly an extrovert, Peter always has something to say.

Down the mountain they come, and we get a glimmer of why Jesus wants secrecy about the big reveal. He orders the three to tell no one what they had seen until after the Son of Man has risen from the dead. Jesus thus considers the timing of the big revelations to be crucial. We might suppose that he does not want to dilute the impact of the resurrection. We might also consider that he knows if this gets around to the authorities, it will complicate and possibly confound what he wishes to do through his death. Peter, James, and John go along, but they still don't understand as

The Executive Summary

Mark reports them "questioning what this rising from the dead could mean." As we surmised in reading chapter 8, Jesus knows that he is going to need to do a lot of teaching and explaining to get that across to them.

They do have a question that Jesus is willing to answer. They ask why the scribes say Elijah must come first, i.e., before the coming of the Messiah. Jesus replies, but candidly his answer is confusing. He agrees that "Elijah is indeed coming first to restore all things." But then Jesus links his answer to a rhetorical question about how it is that the Son of Man must suffer. And then he says that Elijah *has* come and seems to justify this proposition by noting how Elijah was mistreated "as it is written about him." So, Elijah is coming but has already come. The expectation about him is true but not. And there seems to be a suggestion that the coming of Elijah is somehow inconsistent with what Jesus forecasts will happen to the Son of Man, i.e., him.

Mark then presents the healing interlude. Jesus and the three return to the rest of the disciples and find them arguing with the scribes in the midst of a crowd. Jesus wants to know what's going on, and a father brings his son to Jesus. The boy has an unclean spirit. (The symptoms sound a lot like epilepsy.) It turns out the disciples tried to cast out the spirit, but couldn't. Jesus commands the spirit to leave. Evidently, this one is a tough nut to crack since the boy looks dead afterwards. However, Jesus lifts him up, and "he was able to stand."

Jesus's comments to the father prior to the healing and to the disciples afterwards are different from previous instances of this sort. To begin with, Jesus is not compassionate; he is exasperated: "You faithless generation, how much longer must I be among you? How much longer must I put up with you?" The father pleads for Jesus's help "if you are able to do anything." Jesus's reaction accelerates from exasperation to sarcasm and offense: "If you are able!" he says. Then, however, he makes the point he has been positing about the necessity and power of faith: "All things can be done for the one who believes." The father says that he does, and with the predicate of faith again established the healing happens. Afterwards, the disciples ask why they failed to cast out the spirit. Jesus's reply is enigmatic: "This kind can come out only through prayer." This is odd since there was no description or even suggestion of Jesus praying. Rather, he said to the spirit, "I command you." Jesus's answer also indicates that there are gradations—differences—among the unclean spirits. Note too that this one did not recognize Jesus as others had. Moreover, since the disciples had successfully cast out demons when Jesus sent them out in chapter 6, this episode shows that they have more to learn if they are to be fully capable on this score after Jesus is gone. Even another healing interlude is preparing them for that day.

 The road trip of Jesus and his disciples continues. They pass through Galilee, and the remainder of chapter 9 is quality time between just Jesus and them. ("He did not want anyone to know it; for he was teaching his disciples.") For the second time, Jesus tells them exactly what is going to happen to him. But the disciples still don't understand and "were afraid to ask him" what he is talking about. They get to Capernaum. In "the house"—which house? Jesus's?—he asks them "What were you arguing about on the way?" I have to believe that Jesus had a twinkle in his eye as he did so since Mark explains that the disciples on the way had "argued with one another who was the greatest." Jesus probably knew well what they had been doing. In the face of Jesus calling them on it, "they were silent." In other words, they shut up in front of the boss.

 Mark's compression of this latest installment of the road trip, meant to set up additional teachings from Jesus to the twelve, makes me, at least, stop and imagine the disciples' argument on the way. We know that they were contending about who was the greatest. And they were, as I have pointed out, a bunch of Jewish guys. The comic potential of the insults that must have been flying as they figuratively threw elbows at each other and vied for precedence, notwithstanding their ignorance, is rich. Think Mel Brooks.

 The disciples' behavior sets up a teachable moment with Jesus. He offers a series of aphorisms, instructions, and admonitions. They include some of his most famous sayings, many of which have passed into common discourse:

The Executive Summary

- Whoever wants to be first must be last of all and servant of all.
- (With a child in his arms) Whoever welcomes one such child in my name welcomes me.
- Whoever is not against us is for us.
- Salt is good, but if it has lost is saltiness, what good is it?
- Have salt in yourselves.

Yet, this train of teachings poses difficulties on a close reading. They seem elliptical. The first point about first and last is clearly a response to the disciples' ego assertions. But how do the other teachings proceed from that point? In addition, where did the child come from? The reader has been given to understand that Jesus and the disciples were having some private time. The gentleness of the moment with the child also gives way to a violent set of admonitions that begins with self-drowning if one puts a stumbling block in the way of little ones believing in Jesus, and continues with various self-mutilations if one's members get in the way of entering the kingdom of God. Even the salt metaphor is somewhat inscrutable. It begins with everyone being salted with fire, cautions against losing saltiness, urging having salt in ourselves, and being at peace with one another. This is Zen-like. But overall, how is all this linked? What is the logic leading from one teaching to another? As chapter 9 ends, the reader begins to have sympathy for the disciples' lack of understanding.

10

On to Jerusalem

> *They were on the road, going up to Jerusalem, and Jesus was walking ahead of them; they were amazed, and those who followed were afraid. He took the twelve aside again and began to tell them what was to happen to him, saying, "See, we are going up to Jerusalem, and the Son of Man will be handed over to the chief priests and the scribes, and they will condemn him to death; then they will hand him over to the Gentiles; they will mock him, and spit upon him, and flog him, and kill him; and after three days he will rise again."* (Mark 10:32–34)

CHAPTER 10 IS A summing up before Jesus turns toward Jerusalem, the Passion, and the fulfillment of his mission. He has another debate with the Pharisees who again are a foil for his teaching. This exchange concerns divorce. Jesus acknowledges the precept of Moses that allowed a man to divorce his wife by observing certain formalities. (Once again, Jesus knows his Jewish law.) But he goes further and focuses on the heart of the law, which is "the heart." Jesus says that the out Moses allowed was because of the "hardness of heart" that the Pharisees and others show. He makes it clear that at its heart God's commandment does *not* permit the separation of man and wife, and later, with just his disciples, he says that marriages after divorce are adultery.

The Executive Summary

Jesus returns to the distinction between formal, law-based commandments and the heart of the law and commandments with the rich man who asks, sincerely and respectfully, how he can inherit eternal life. Jesus cites the commandments, the foundation of Jewish law, and the rich man says he has kept them. But he has missed their essence—their heart. Jesus makes this clear by telling the rich man he lacks only one thing—to relinquish all his material success to the poor and to follow Jesus. Note that in this instance, Jesus is not critical of the rich man; Mark says that Jesus "loved him" as he explains the heart of what God wants. This is all tough stuff for twenty-first century ears.

Other encounters in this chapter reprise and amplify earlier teachings. Despite what Jesus told his disciples about children in Chapter 9, they "sternly" tried to keep people from bringing little children to Jesus for his blessing. Jesus was "indignant" and uses this episode to say more about the kingdom of God. It "belongs" to "such as these" and whoever does not "receive" it "as a little child" will not "enter" it. The kingdom of God is thus about membership. Some may enter it, and some will not. The qualifications for entry include simplicity and sincerity. What is not mentioned are qualities that society values—cunning, intelligence, slickness, toughness, and material success. Jesus underscores this when the disciples react to his instruction to the rich man and his statement that it will be hard for the wealthy to enter the kingdom of God.

We also hear another version of the teaching about family in Chapter 3. Peter, the extrovert, cannot contain himself in the face of the rich man lesson, and reminds Jesus, somewhat cheekily, that he and others *have* left everything to follow Jesus. Jesus's answer is nuanced. He says that those who have left their natural families behind for his sake and the sake of the good news will receive "a hundredfold" now and "eternal life" in the age to come. But the rewards in this age will include "persecutions." He reiterates that "many who are first will be last, and the last will be first." Not to be deterred, James and John press Jesus to be allowed places of honor next to him "in his glory." They still want to be "the greatest."

Of course, the other ten disciples are angry when they hear this. Jesus disdainfully compares the request of James and John to the behavior of the Gentiles—Jesus remains a faithful Jew—and says again that following him means servanthood to others, just as he is doing. The disciples still have a hard time getting it.

We learn about the nature of God from Jesus in this chapter. It is God who makes people male and female—not our choice. It is God who joins man and wife together—again, not our choice. No one is good but God alone—not even, he says, himself. It is God's decision who will be saved—for mortals it is impossible. Who will get to be with Jesus is not up to him—it is "for those for whom it has been prepared," i.e., by God.

In chapter 10, we have one more healing. This time it is a blind beggar in Jericho. The crowd at first tells him not to bother Jesus, but Jesus calls him. The people tell the blind man to "take heart"—there is the heart again. When he addresses Jesus as his "teacher," Jesus tells him his faith has made him well, and he regains his sight and follows Jesus. Faith again is the key.

Mark names the blind beggar—Bartimaeus, son of Timaeus. Why is he singled out? Perhaps it is because he identifies Jesus in a new way, not seen in Mark before. Twice, he calls Jesus "Son of David." David, of course, was another of the most important figures in Jewish history, the founding King of Israel, anointed by God. Through his story in the Books of Samuel, we learn about what kingship of God's people entails and therefore more clues about the kingdom of God. We also learn that God had made David's house and kingship "steadfast forever" and his "throne unshaken forever." If Jesus is Son of David, he is part of that house and heir to this unshaken kingship.

The journey of Jesus and the disciples goes on in chapter 10, but it takes a decisive turn. They have crossed into Judea and are going up to Jerusalem. Jesus is leading them and other followers. They are "amazed" and "afraid." They must sense danger. Given the ongoing conflict with the Pharisees and scribes throughout Mark and Jesus's remarkable teachings that, among other things, were likely to provoke the established authorities, that would not

The Executive Summary

be surprising. One more time, Jesus tells the twelve what is going to happen to him. This is the third time that he has done so. The threefold pattern reappears.

11

Jerusalem: Throwing the Gauntlet

When they were approaching Jerusalem, at Bethphage and Bethany, near the Mount of Olives, he sent two of his disciples and said to them, "Go into the village ahead of you, and immediately as you enter it, you will find tied there a colt that has never been ridden; untie it and bring it. . . . Then they brought the colt to Jesus and threw their cloaks on it; and he sat on it. Many people spread their cloaks on the road, and others spread leafy branches that they had cut in the fields. Then those who went ahead and those who followed were shouting,
  "Hosanna!
  Blessed is the one who comes in the name of the Lord!
  Blessed is the coming kingdom of our ancestor David!
  Hosanna in the highest heaven!"
  . . . Then they came to Jerusalem. And he entered the temple and began to drive out those who were selling and those who were buying in the temple, and he overturned the tables of the money changers and the seats of those who sold doves; and he would not allow anyone to carry anything through the temple. He was teaching and saying, "Is it not written,
  'My house shall be called a house of prayer for all the nations'?
  But you have made it a den of robbers."
  And when the chief priests and the scribes heard it, they kept looking for a way to kill him; for they were

The Executive Summary

afraid of him, because the whole crowd was spellbound by his teaching. And when evening came, Jesus and his disciples went out of the city. . . . Again they came to Jerusalem. As he was walking in the temple, the chief priests, the scribes, and the elders came to him and said, "By what authority are you doing these things? Who gave you this authority to do them?" (Mark 11:1–2, 7–10, 15–19, 27–28)

CHAPTER 11 RECOUNTS THE first two days, and part of the third day, of Jesus in Jerusalem. With six chapters remaining, including chapter 11, about one-third of Mark's Gospel deals with this week of Jesus's ministry. To this point it has not been clear how long Jesus has been at work since his baptism by John. Mark is almost completely silent about dating, but it must have been much, much more than a week. Mark's decision to devote roughly one-third of the gospel to Jesus's week in Jerusalem alone tells us the importance Mark places upon it. Moreover, as the week builds, so does the length of Mark's account. Teaching and healing in the provinces were prologue; what happens to Jesus during this week in Jerusalem is the crucial point of the gospel.

On Day One, Jesus and his disciples are approaching Jerusalem. Mark is very specific about where they are: at Bethpage and Bethany, nearing the Mount of Olives. Jesus then sends two of the disciples, unnamed, to the "village ahead" of them, also unnamed, to get the "colt" for him to ride. Jesus supplies the disciples with a way to deflect villagers' objections to "borrowing" the colt. This is curious. Why the details in some respects and not others? For that matter, why any detail at all of how he got the colt? It puts him in a less than flattering light. The colt has to belong to somebody, and Jesus is just taking it with a somewhat misleading story (to the village bystanders at least). He does, however, promise to return it, and presumably did.

The real significance of the story about the colt is how Jesus has chosen to enter Jerusalem. Here, translation is important. The traditional one for the animal, in my experience, is "donkey" or "ass." "Colt" is less specific (and squares with the age of the animal since it had "never been ridden"). It could be a young horse, donkey, or mule. I am inclined to think it was the latter—a mule. My reason is that at the time of King David, royal personages—kings and princes—rode mules. It was a symbol of their royal status. Recall that the blind beggar at the end of chapter 10 shouted out to Jesus that he was "Son of David." If Jesus is now claiming kingship, it would make sense for him to enter Jerusalem on a mule. It would also make sense that the crowd would understand the symbolism of the mule, and to make the connection that a king, a descendant of David, was arriving. And indeed, in chapter 11, the crowd shouts to Jesus as he rides to Jerusalem, "Blessed is the coming kingdom of our ancestor David!" Recall the first quoted words of Jesus in chapter 1: "the kingdom of God has come near."

In the face of all this, Day One ends with a bit of anticlimax. Mark reports that upon entering Jerusalem, Jesus goes to the temple, looks around, and heads back out of the city to Bethany. This feels like a letdown at the culmination of a royal procession. On the other hand, as far as we know from Mark, this is the first time that Jesus has ever been to the temple. So, it may be reasonable under those circumstances for him simply to take stock of this critical venue, the focal point of God's relationship to humanity.

Day Two begins with another curious detail. Jesus is hungry, sees a fig tree, finds it has no figs, and curses it. Given what Jesus knows lies ahead of him, perhaps he was a little edgy? In any event, Mark is at pains to note that the disciples heard his curse of the tree. This sets up Peter's realization at the beginning of Day Three that the fig tree has withered, and one more teaching moment from Jesus about the vital importance of faith. If they, and we, "[h]ave faith in God . . . whatever you ask for in prayer . . . will be yours." But this comes with a qualification: "Whenever you stand praying, forgive . . . so that your Father in heaven may also forgive you." Once again, as at the beginning of his ministry and his first quoted words: repent, believe.

The heart of Day Two, however, is the return to the temple, the overturning of the tables of the moneychangers and others commercializing the temple, and the coming conflict with the chief priests and scribes. As at the end of Day One, Jesus and the disciples leave the city when evening arrives. Why don't they stay in Jerusalem?

On Day Three, Jesus and disciples are back in Jerusalem and the temple. The chief priests, scribes, and elders confront him, and the gravamen of their complaint is authority—"By what authority" is he acting? Jesus's answers their question with a question—a very Jewish argumentative mode—and invokes John the Baptist. This too takes us back to where we, and Jesus, began at the outset of the gospel, and links him to this Jewish religious leader. Note too that when Peter addresses Jesus about the withered fig tree, it is as "Rabbi." Jesus has not stopped being a Jew even as he heads toward the crucifixion and rising he has foretold. Jesus's confrontation with the Jewish religious authorities on this day and the rest of the week remains an argument within, and not against, Judaism.

All of chapter 11 is about authority. Jesus claims it as a king with the manner of his entry into Jerusalem. The crowds recognize his authority with their exclamations linking him to David and their "spellbound" reaction to his teaching. He asserts his authority in the temple as he chases away the moneychangers. The chief priests et al., realize this and explicitly question him about it. He deflects their question, but the king has thrown the gauntlet.

12

Jerusalem: Routing the Establishment

> *One of the scribes came near and heard them disputing with one another, and seeing that he answered them well, he asked him, "Which commandment is the first of all?" Jesus answered, "The first is, 'Hear, O Israel: the Lord our God, the Lord is one; you shall love the Lord your God with all your heart, and with all your soul, and with all your mind, and with all your strength.' The second is this, 'You shall love your neighbor as yourself.' There is no other commandment greater than these." Then the scribe said to him, "You are right, Teacher; you have truly said that 'he is one, and besides him there is no other'; and 'to love him with all the heart, and with all the understanding, and with all the strength,' and 'to love one's neighbor as oneself,'—this is much more important than all whole burnt offerings and sacrifices." When Jesus saw that he answered wisely, he said to him, "You are not far from the kingdom of God." After that no one dared to ask him any question.* (Mark 12:28–34)

DAY THREE CONTINUES IN chapter 12 along with Jesus's confrontation with the establishment religious authorities. He teaches, and some of his lessons are pointed. They include a number of sayings that have become aphorisms in Western culture.

The first teaching is effectively Jesus's answer to the challenge to his authority by the chief priests, elders, and scribes that ended

The Executive Summary

chapter 11. He tells the parable of the vineyard, the attempt of the owner to collect his share from the tenants, and the tenants' abuse and killing of the owner's representatives, including his own son. The parable's conclusion is that the owner will destroy the tenants and give the vineyard to others. Quoting Psalm 118:22, Jesus adds the twist that "The stone that the builders rejected has become the cornerstone." This had to outrage the establishment authorities. It's not hard to see that they are the "tenants" that God, "the owner," will destroy, and that Jesus is the cornerstone that they are rejecting but that God will utilize. And indeed, on top of their earlier desire to kill him, Mark reports that they want to arrest Jesus but do not because they fear the crowd.

The authorities have another go at Jesus by sending "some Pharisees and some Herodians to trap him." One can imagine the religious leaders storming back to the equivalent of their office and fuming. Some of their associates and underlings would have been all too ready to enter the fray. After all, they were learned and sophisticated. They had a great chance to curry favor with the big shots. They must also have felt contempt for the hick from the provinces: "Let me at this phony. I'll tie him in knots!" (The disdain that Easterners in 1860 had for Abraham Lincoln, the prairie galoot, gives us an idea of their likely reaction to Jesus.) This new gambit also begins to move the conflict from the religious to the political arena. The involvement of the Herodians signals this. And the question they put to Jesus about the lawfulness of paying taxes to the emperor confirms it. (The false unctuousness of their approach to Jesus betrays their belief that they can easily outsmart him.) Jesus, however, is ready and plays rope-a-dope. Taking a Roman coin with the likeness of Caesar, he says: "Give to the emperor the things that are the emperor's, and to God the things that are God's." Explain that riposte to your bosses!

Next up are the Sadducees with a brain twister about a man with seven brothers, his widow, serial marriages without children, and the resurrection. In response, Jesus offers an insight about life after the resurrection; the whole point is that it is not like life on earth. He also quotes the book of Moses in which God speaks from the burning bush in the present tense to show that He is the God of the living, i.e., of Abraham, Isaac, and Jacob, and not of the dead.

One of the scribes takes a final shot and asks which commandment is first of all. Jesus answers by reciting the *Shema* and adds a commandment to love your neighbor as yourself. The scribe throws in the towel: "You are right, Teacher . . . this is much more important than all whole burnt offerings and sacrifices." I would not have bet much on that scribe's job security.

And so, Jesus has verbally routed all his establishment adversaries. Given the awful way Jesus's crucifixion has been used against the Jews over the centuries, I am at pains to point out, once again, how Jesus has resorted to Jewish Scriptures in his duels with the establishment religious authorities and how the crowd in the temple—undoubtedly all Jews—"was listening to him with delight."

He goes on teaching in the temple. In one of his admonitions, he leaves no doubt of how little he thinks of the authorities: "Beware of the scribes . . . They will receive the greater condemnation." It is hard to escape the conclusion that Jesus was asking for it. He had taken on the establishment on their home ground—the sacred space of the temple. Of course, they would come after him and get rid of him. He had predicted it, three times to his disciples. The authorities could not afford not to.

But what of it? The key would be the resurrection. Could he really rise from the dead? If not, he would be just another failed agitator and challenger to the established order. If so, he would prove that he was the Anointed One. On this score, he made a crucial distinction to the crowd in the temple. The Messiah, he said, citing Jewish Scripture, is not going to be a son of David and, therefore, not a king like David. The kingdom of God, to which Jesus had been pointing from the very beginning, is going to be different.

13

Jerusalem: The Shape of Things to Come

As he came out of the temple, one of his disciples said to him, "Look, Teacher, what large stones and what large buildings!" Then Jesus asked him, "Do you see these great buildings? Not one stone will be left here upon another; all will be thrown down." When he was sitting on the Mount of Olives opposite the temple, Peter, James, John, and Andrew asked him privately, "Tell us, when will this be, and what will be the sign that all these things are about to be accomplished?" Then Jesus began to say to them, "Beware that no one leads you astray. Many will come in my name and say, 'I am he!' and they will lead many astray. When you hear of wars and rumors of wars, do not be alarmed; this must take place, but the end is still to come. For nation will rise against nation, and kingdom against kingdom; there will be earthquakes in various places; there will be famines. This is but the beginning of the birth pangs. . . .
But in those days, after that suffering,
  the sun will be darkened,
  and the moon will not give its light,
  and the stars will be falling from heaven,
  and the powers in the heavens will be shaken.
Then they will see 'the Son of Man coming in clouds' with great power and glory. Then he will send out the angels, and gather his elect from the four winds, from the ends of

> the earth to the ends of heaven. . . . Truly I tell you, this generation will not pass away until all these things have taken place. Heaven and earth will pass away, but my words will not pass away. But about that day or hour no one knows, neither the angels in heaven, nor the Son, but only the Father. Beware, keep alert; for you do not know when the time will come." (Mark 13:1–8, 24–27, 30–33)

THE ENTIRETY OF CHAPTER 13 consists of Jesus's prophecy about the future—what will happen after he is gone and the conditions that will prefigure the Son of Man's return and the end of heaven and earth. It too contains turns of phrase that have entered popular discourse (e.g., "wars and rumors of war"; "nation will rise against nation"; "false Messiahs and false prophets"). For the portion of the gospel meant to foretell the future, however, it leaves many questions unanswered.

It begins with Jesus coming out of the temple, so we are still in Day Three. But after Jesus predicts the destruction of the temple in reaction to the gee-whiz admiration of its size by one of the disciples, the scene quickly shifts to the Mount of Olives, outside the city but overlooking the temple. The disciple's exclamation about the temple is a little curious since the disciples had been to the temple three times at that point; the disciple's wonder at it would have made sense earlier. In any event, when Jesus sits at the Mount of Olives, it is not clear if we are still in Day Three—an awful lot has taken place. But we probably are since the next chapter (14) begins with the statement that it was two days before Passover, which if it began at sundown on Thursday would mean that Day Three (Tuesday) was not over when Chapter 14 begins or, therefore, as Jesus began his prophecy. One other point of interest before we address the prophecy itself is that Jesus delivers it "privately" to another inside circle of disciples—Peter, James, and John, who have been so privileged before, and now Andrew, who gets to join the executive session. These were the original four that Jesus called.

It begins with the four asking when will "this" be and what will be the sign that "these things" are about to be accomplished. The only occurrence that Jesus has spoken about of this nature so

The Executive Summary

far is the temple's destruction. This would have been an apocalyptic development for Jews. The temple contained the Ark of the Covenant, and was the place where God himself could be accessed, the spiritual junction of heaven and earth. This is the question that Jesus addresses.

He makes the following predictions:

- The first signs are wars, earthquakes, and famines—"the beginning of the birth pangs." "Birth pangs" suggests that something is going to be created and not just destroyed.
- Jesus's followers will suffer badly, but those who endure to the end will be saved. He offers some advice to this end: The good news must be proclaimed to all nations, and when his followers are put on trial, they should not worry about what to say. The Holy Spirit will guide them.
- The real trigger will be when "the desolating sacrilege [is] set up where it ought not to be." And Mark's Gospel adds "(let the reader understand)." At that point the real suffering will take place, "such as has not been from the beginning of the creation."
- False messiahs and prophets will appear. They will try to lead his followers astray. He makes this point twice.
- After the great suffering, the Son of Man will come in the clouds and gather "his elect."

This account in Mark's Gospel presents a number of difficulties. Jesus repeatedly tells Peter, James, John, and Andrew to "beware." First of all, why just these four? Shouldn't all the disciples have been briefed? In addition, despite Jesus saying that "I have told you everything," if I were them, I would be a little uncertain. How are we to tell if someone is a false messiah or false prophet? Moreover, resorting to a fig tree metaphor (I guess he was still ticked at the tree with no figs), Jesus says that when you see the things that he has predicted taking place, you will know "he," i.e., the Son of Man, "is near." But I thought Jesus was the Son of Man. Here, he seems to be talking about someone else. Or perhaps he is speaking about himself in the third person and means a transformation of himself into this figure.

Most disconcertingly, Jesus then says "Truly I tell you, this generation will not pass away until all these things have taken place." Well, that just did not happen. The temple was destroyed during the lifetime of his disciples, but the Son of Man did not appear and heaven and earth did not pass away as he predicted. True, Jesus did give himself an out when he immediately next said that "about that day or hour no one knows, neither the angels in heaven, nor the Son, but only the Father." With an analogy to a master leaving his house and putting others in charge, he admonishes the four disciples, and us, to "keep awake.'" But how and still function and survive in daily life? It's been 2,000 years. And what are we looking for? The temple has been destroyed already, and there are no prospects that it will be rebuilt any time soon. And what would the "desolating sacrilege" be to us? The aside from either Mark or Jesus to "let the reader understand" really does not help.

There are also some oddities in his description of the timing of these events and the separation between the Father and the Son. During the time of great suffering, Jesus says, "Pray that it may not be in Winter." So, Jesus does not know the season when the suffering will take place. He then says that "if the Lord *had* not cut short the days, no one would be saved." (My emphasis.) He also says that "for the sake of the elect, whom he chose, he *has* cut short those days." (My emphasis again.) This suggests it has already happened. However, what Jesus has been giving is prophecy—what is *yet* to happen. Like Jesus's caveat above about when all that he predicts will take place, he distances himself from the Father in making these points. The introduction of the elect into this end-time scenario is disconcerting too. Have the survivors already been identified? Can some not be saved even if they choose to keep the commandments and follow what Jesus has been teaching? Perhaps the answers are to be found beyond our understanding of time. We think in linear time, but God stands outside time. Jesus begins to give us a sense of that in chapter 13.

14

Jerusalem: Passover

While they were eating, he took a loaf of bread, and after blessing it he broke it, gave it to them, and said, "Take; this is my body." Then he took a cup, and after giving thanks he gave it to them, and all of them drank from it. He said to them, "This is my blood of the covenant, which is poured out for many. Truly I tell you, I will never again drink of the fruit of the vine until that day when I drink it new in the kingdom of God." (Mark 14:22–25)

THE STORY OF JESUS moves quickly toward its climax in this chapter. It is time-stamped as "two days before the Passover and the festival of Unleavened Bread." Since we know that the Passover meal between Jesus and his disciples was Thursday night, this would mean that Passover began at sundown on Thursday and that therefore chapter 14 begins late in the day on Tuesday. The festival of Unleavened Bread in ancient Israel was a related, but separate, event that began at sundown on the day following Passover and lasted a week. This will introduce a timing difficulty later in the chapter, as we will see.

In any event, chapter 14 begins with Mark reporting that the chief priests and scribes were scheming to arrest Jesus by stealth and kill him. It continues at a fast-moving pace: to Bethany where Jesus dines, to Judas striking a deal with the religious authorities to betray Jesus, to the "first day of Unleavened Bread when the

JERUSALEM: PASSOVER

Passover lamb is sacrificed," to the Passover meal (which we have come to call the Last Supper), to the Mount of Olives, to Gethsemane and "immediately" Judas's betrayal leading to Jesus's arrest, to Jesus's interrogation and religious trial in the house of the high priest, and to Peter's denial.

Along the way, Mark gives us a number of specific and somewhat unexpected details. From a literary perspective, one could say they provide verisimilitude. From a historical perspective, they add to one's confidence that Mark is telling about something that in fact happened. They include:

- Jesus does not just dine in Bethany. He sits at table in the house of "Simon the leper." (Who is he? Perhaps this is just his fifteen seconds of fame.) And while there, a curious thing happens. A woman, unidentified, anoints Jesus (lavishly) with costly ointment, nard.

- When Jesus's disciples ask for directions on preparing the Passover meal, Jesus tells two of them to go into the city and there a man carrying a jug of water will meet them. They are to follow him to a house where there will be a guest room for the meal. Lo and behold, just like the directions about the colt for the entry into Jerusalem, the two (again two and unidentified) find just what Jesus described and do as he instructed.

- As Jesus is arrested, someone, presumably on his side, draws a sword and cuts off the ear of the slave of the high priest.

- As the arrest happens, all of the disciples bug out, but a young man, unidentified and just wearing a linen cloth, follows Jesus. The posse carrying out the arrest catches hold of him, but he leaves the cloth behind and runs away naked. (What a mental image!)

The events of chapter 14 present us with an over-arching difficulty. To someone with a lifetime in the church, the story has been heard and read so many times that it is hard to think about it anew. I have attempted this (as I have throughout this commentary) and noted some points that I, at least, had not picked up before.

The Executive Summary

One is the issue of dates and timing, alluded to above. If I am correct about the chapter beginning Tuesday, probably late in the day, and ending Thursday night, very late, what happened to Wednesday? What were Jesus and the disciples doing then? Possibly Judas went to the chief priests with his offer of betrayal that day, but is that it? Maybe Jesus took the day off from teaching in the temple, and instead was doing his own preparations for Passover (thus accounting for his specific instructions to the two disciples about the man with the water jar). But this seems odd given Jesus's mission and its culmination in Jerusalem. Another timing discontinuity concerns the preparations themselves. Mark says that these were on the "first day of Unleavened Bread when the Passover lamb is sacrificed." But the festival of Unleavened Bread began the day *after* Passover and was distinct from it. My understanding is that the temple priests were busy with sacrificing lambs for Passover on the day before Passover, so the latter part of this assertion in Mark makes sense. But not the first part. Perhaps this is a clue that Mark was a Gentile who confused these two related observances, although his knowledge of Jewish Scripture and practices is otherwise impressive.

Money figures into consecutive passages early in the chapter. First, the disciples are indignant at the woman's waste in anointing Jesus with nard. They observe that it could have been sold for a considerable sum ("more than three hundred denarii," another telling detail) and used to provide for the poor. Jesus puts them off. She has done him a "good service," they can always show kindness to the poor but they won't have him for long, and she has anointed his body for burial beforehand. (And recall that kings, like David, are anointed; Jesus is about to establish his kingship.) Then Mark shifts to Judas going to the chief priests to betray Jesus. Mark reports that they were greatly pleased and promised to give Judas money. So, money is dismissed even for charity, but it is taken for betrayal (indeed, *the* betrayal of all time). There is irony here and a subtle lesson not to value money.

Another irony is the conduct of the disciples themselves. Jesus warns them that that they all will become "deserters." This prompts

Peter's famous protestation: "Even though I must die with you, I will not deny you," and "all of them said the same." When Jesus is arrested, however, "[a]ll of them deserted him and fled." And of course, in typical bombastic fashion, Peter denies Jesus three times before the cock crows twice, and then poignantly realizes what he has done, and breaks down and weeps.

The three-fold pattern seen earlier in the gospel occurs again. Peter denies Jesus three times as Jesus predicted he would. And earlier at Gethsemane when Jesus gathers his inner circle of Peter, James, and John (no Andrew this time) and goes off to pray prior to the arrest and death he knows is coming, he returns three times only to find the three of them sleeping.

More ironies occur at the trial in the high priest's house. The chief priests and council stumble around and search for various gotchas, and fail. (Who were "the many" who gave false and conflicting testimony that night? Probably the usual flunkies and weasels who are drawn to and useful to those in power.) After all the verbal duels between Jesus and religious leaders throughout the gospel, the issue is finally decided by a simple direct question and direct answer. The high priest asks Jesus if he is the Messiah, the Son of the Blessed One, and Jesus says "I am." (Referencing the Book of Daniel, Jesus throws in "the Son of Man seated at the right hand of the Power and coming with the clouds of heaven.") This simple resolution is itself ironic given the twists and turns that preceded it and because it is Jesus's own words that convict him and nothing that the religious authorities ferret out. And the high priest adds one more hypocritical irony. He tears his clothes upon Jesus's answer. This is an ancient practice associated with sorrow and mourning at the loss of a loved one. Of course, the high priest is not sorrowful at all; he has gotten what he wanted—the ability to condemn Jesus and get him out of the way.

For all of this, the most important portion of chapter 14 is the Passover meal. Jesus and the disciples are very traditional in observing it, right up to singing "the hymn" at the end. While it is not clear what hymn this is, singing by the participants after the meal is a Passover tradition down to the present day. (I wonder what

The Executive Summary

kind of voice Jesus and some of the others had.) During the Passover meal, Jesus institutes the central element of Christian worship observed ever since—the Eucharist, the bread and wine that he states are his body and blood. Christian worship, but founded on the Jewish Passover. And the key part of the meal, the sacrificial lamb, is replaced by Jesus, who is sacrificing himself "for many." Once again, a Jewish base with an addition that Jesus provides. Indeed, to the end, Jesus continues to operate within Judaism. He celebrates the Passover, he references Zechariah when he says that the shepherd will be struck and the sheep scattered, and he quotes Daniel to the high priest. Even Judas, at the moment of betrayal, addresses him as "Rabbi."

There is a sense of inevitability to chapter 14—no real surprises—even when read with fresh eyes. Jesus has been predicting what would happen for a good while. He came to Jerusalem and goaded the religious authorities. Judas betrayed him, but somehow or other Jesus was going to get arrested, tried, and condemned. He himself even gives the high priest what he needs after the high priest and his cronies flounder around at the trial. The real suspense still lies ahead. Jesus says to his disciples, "after I am raised up, I will go before you to Galilee." Will he really be able to do that? If he can, the implications are enormous.

15

Jerusalem: Death

> *As soon as it was morning, the chief priests held a consultation with the elders and scribes and the whole council. They bound Jesus, led him away, and handed him over to Pilate. Pilate asked him, "Are you the King of the Jews?" He answered him, "You say so." Then the chief priests accused him of many things. Pilate asked him again, "Have you no answer? See how many charges they bring against you." But Jesus made no further reply, so that Pilate was amazed. . . . It was nine o'clock in the morning when they crucified him. The inscription of the charge against him read, "The King of the Jews."* (Mark 15:1–5, 25–26)

THE CRUCIFIXION AND DEATH of Jesus, recounted in chapter 15, present the same general problem as the account in chapter 14. The material is so well known that in reading it one sweeps along and risks not focusing on salient points. It is easy for one's mind to say: "Yes, yes, I know all this, move on." As with chapter 14, I have tried to read this chapter deliberately and afresh.

In sum, the chief priests and other religious establishment figures take Jesus to Pilate. He asks Jesus a few questions, puts him before "the crowd" at "the festival," and poses who he should release—Jesus or Barabbas. They shout for Jesus to be crucified and not Barabbas. That seals the deal, and Pilate hands Jesus over to the Roman troops for crucifixion.

The Executive Summary

Let's dig deeper and draw some reasonable inferences about this sequence. Note that the first thing the chief priests did at daybreak was to hold a "consultation with the elders and scribes and the whole council." They probably decided that Pilate wouldn't care about whether Jesus was claiming to be the Messiah and blasphemy; that's Jewish stuff. But he would care if Jesus was claiming to be a king; that's political and a threat to Rome. Of course, someone claiming to be the Messiah would be *the* king to Jews. So, without doing violence to their position, the temple leaders shift the accusation just a bit to something that would get Pilate's attention.

Since they act "as soon as it was morning," the chief priests et al., likely roused Pilate out of bed, and he was likely annoyed. It was the crack of dawn. Yes, it's very early, but they have got their man and the Sabbath begins that day at sundown. So, they want to move quickly. One can imagine a grumpy Pilate hearing the accusation and groggily trying to interrogate Jesus. Another aspect of this is that Pilate is probably speaking Latin, and Jesus Aramaic. So, someone would have to translate; this would hinder much back-and-forth. Pilate wants to get to the heart of the matter from his perspective. He would be concerned about sedition; is this guy another Jewish troublemaker? After all, that's Pilate's prime job—to keep the peace and maintain Roman rule. (Jumping a bit ahead, the description of Barabbas as "one of the rebels who committed murder during the insurrection" is telling; trouble can always be brewing.) So, his question, "Are you the King of the Jews?" makes sense. Jesus deflects this. Recognizing from bitter experience that this clever rabbi may be about to slip the leash, the chief priests start interjecting. One can imagine Pilate eyeing them and then asking Jesus, in essence, "what do you have to say about all that?" Jesus doesn't answer, which surprises Pilate. Mark says that he was "amazed."

By now Pilate would be fully awake and on his game. Jesus's refusal to answer has him ready for conviction—forget about innocent until proven guilty in this so-called court. From Pilate's point of view, it's the other way around, especially if the temple leaders are doing the accusing. Again, what Pilate wants is to maintain order. Even if he senses that they are trying to get rid of a rival as Mark reports, he can't risk sending them away angry; they might cause trouble. That is what could then get Pilate into hot water with his Roman lords and masters.

Pilate is a shrewd and cynical Roman functionary, even a little sadistic. That is how I read Pilate's interaction with the crowd and his final decision. For one thing, remember that it is still early in the morning at this point. Later, when Jesus is actually crucified, Mark says that it is nine o'clock in the morning. What with everything that happens up to then (the soldiers torturing and mocking Jesus and marching him out of the city to Golgotha), Pilate's banter with the crowd has to be well earlier than 9 a.m. And it *is* banter on Pilate's part—disingenuous and sarcastic questions that imply Pilate's contempt for them. And let's think about who would be in "the crowd" at that hour of the morning—not the general Jewish public, but probably more of the flunkies and weasels that help the temple leaders with necessary dirty work. Mark says that "the chief priests stirred up the crowd," a far easier task with those whom I envision. As far as Pilate is concerned, this has been sort of fun, but he really doesn't care. Order Jesus's crucifixion. Maybe he really is a troublemaker. Roman rule has to be maintained. Another dead Jew. So what? Time for breakfast.

With Pilate's order, Jesus's crucifixion becomes a completely Roman operation. The Roman soldiers, undoubtedly a rough lot in a garrison far from home and in a place they don't like, decide to have some sport. To them Jesus is a powerless loser, so some torture and serious ridicule are in order. They then march Jesus out, and they, i.e., the Romans, crucify him. As he did in chapter 14, Mark gives us some details not necessary to the account but bolstering its authenticity. A specific person, "Simon of Cyrene, father of Alexander and Rufus," is a passer-by, coming in from the country, and is compelled by the soldiers to carry Jesus's cross. Jesus refuses wine mixed with myrrh, a concoction to lessen pain. Once Jesus is on the cross, Mark notes that there were women who had followed him looking on from a distance. They are named— Mary Magdalene and Mary "the mother of James the younger and of Joses, and of Salome." This latter appears to be the mother of one of the twelve. Jesus's mother is not named.

Mark's description of the death of Jesus offers one poignant note and two discordant ones. The former is Jesus's cry, "'*Eloi, Eloi, lema sabachthani?*' which means, "My God, my God, why have you forsaken me?" (Another hint that Mark was a Gentile as he saw the need to translate.) These are the only quoted words of Jesus on the cross in Mark. On the surface it is a statement of abject frustration and dereliction. But Jesus is referencing Psalm 22 which begins with this bitter lament, aptly describes what he is going through, and builds to a statement of faith. Quoting a psalm attributed to King David, Jesus was indeed a Jew until he breathed his last and did not lose faith. The discordant notes are the assertion that the curtain of the temple—which shielded the holy of holies—was then torn in two, and the statement of the centurion that "Truly this man was God's son!" The former feels like something inserted for dramatic effect. The latter seems highly unlikely given the soldiers' behavior toward Jesus and their ongoing duties. This was not the first Jewish "criminal" that they would crucify and probably not the last.

Finally, we have Joseph of Arimathea, a "respected member of the council." If he was, he would have been present at the meeting that morning where the chief priests and others got their signals straight before approaching Pilate. Did he voice objections and get overruled? Seeing himself in the minority, did he speak up at all? In any event, maybe motivated by some guilt and perhaps at some risk to himself, he goes "boldly" to Pilate and asks for the body of Jesus. After checking with a centurion to confirm Jesus's death, Pilate grants the request. Why not? Something has to be done with it, and if this guy wants to take it off the Romans' hands, fine. And then there is another telling detail as Joseph lays the body in the tomb. Joseph rolls a stone against the door of the tomb. If Joseph, likely an older man, can do this by himself, it isn't really that hard to move it. But as a mahoff, he could have had some younger helpers.

Chapter 15 thus ends. We have a cliffhanger. Will Jesus rise as he foretold?

16

Resurrection

When the sabbath was over, Mary Magdalene, and Mary the mother of James, and Salome bought spices, so that they might go and anoint him. And very early on the first day of the week, when the sun had risen, they went to the tomb. They had been saying to one another, "Who will roll away the stone for us from the entrance to the tomb?" When they looked up, they saw that the stone, which was very large, had already been rolled back. As they entered the tomb, they saw a young man, dressed in a white robe, sitting on the right side; and they were alarmed. But he said to them, "Do not be alarmed; you are looking for Jesus of Nazareth, who was crucified. He has been raised; he is not here. Look, there is the place they laid him. But go, tell his disciples and Peter that he is going ahead of you to Galilee; there you will see him, just as he told you." So they went out and fled from the tomb, for terror and amazement had seized them; and they said nothing to anyone, for they were afraid. (Mark 16:1–8)

AT FIRST BLUSH, THE ending of Mark's Gospel brings one up short. It is very brief. It is abrupt. It is not a triumphal Easter morning moment. The two Mary's go early on the first day of the week, i.e., Sunday morning after the Sabbath has ended, to anoint the deceased body of Jesus. They are worried about who is going to roll away the "very large" stone—a little odd if Joseph of Arimathea was able to roll it into place by himself. But, as I have noted, he may have had help, and in that society at that time this was probably not a task that women are expected to do. Nevertheless, it does not matter; the stone has been rolled away.

They enter the tomb. A "young man, dressed in a white robe" is sitting there (on the right side, another specific detail). No Jesus. Of course, they are alarmed. The young man in white tells them that Jesus has been raised and can be found in Galilee. Happy ending! He did it! And if we care about inclusion, it is noteworthy that it is the women and not the disciples who first learn of the resurrection.

But there is a twist. The young man tells them to go tell Peter and the other disciples. The women, however, flee: "terror and amazement had seized them." Moreover, "they said nothing to anyone, for they were afraid." And there Mark's Gospel ends.

The abrupt ending suggests that the real ending has gone missing—not all that surprising for ancient sources. The NRSV adds bracketed material that says the women did eventually tell those around Peter, and there is a broad feel-good statement about the spread of the "sacred and imperishable proclamation of eternal salvation." This does not sound like the Mark I have been reading. It is not hard to speculate that someone later felt a need to tidy up the ending. I understand that there have been other addenda in other translations that have the same feel and possible purpose.

But what if the women fleeing, "for they were afraid," is indeed the ending? It sounds like Mark. I have previously suggested that Mark followed good short story-writing principles with the transfers of energy in his narrative. After a complete reading of his gospel, I believe that Mark was Chekhovan—an absence of much authorial commentary and didacticism, brevity, a focus on a few details, gestures, and features that are both precise and elusive, and, most importantly, the formulation of the right questions rather than prescribing the correct solutions. Or perhaps I should say that Chekhov was Markan.

If Mark's Gospel does end this way, it raises the obvious question: Will the women accept the truth? Of course, they must have overcome their fear and did. How else could Mark have written his gospel thirty-to-forty years after the events he describes? But by ending this way, Mark also raises the crucial question for his readers: Will *they* accept the truth and its implications? Will you and I? Think of it this way: Suppose, like the women, we are told by someone authoritative that we can see Jesus. What an opportunity! But, after that initial reaction, I would be astonished and skeptical. And then I would likely become afraid too. What if I did go see him, and he looked me in the eye and said, as he did to the rich young man in chapter 10: "Drop whatever you are doing, sell your possessions, give money to the poor. Follow me." Would I be ready for that? Would you? This would be the question that Mark leaves us with.

Mark's Gospel has laid out who Jesus was and his message. He has stated, through the young man in white (most likely an angel), that Jesus did in fact rise from the dead and do what he said he would do. The implications are huge. This really means that he was the Christ, the anointed one of God. Through him, God brought himself into the world and came looking to help us—to steer us back into the right path and to save us. God had provided the markers for this through his Chosen People and the Commandments, the Prophets, and Jewish Scripture. But we needed more, and God gave it to us with Jesus. Mark is telling us that the time is fulfilled, and it is up to us to overcome our fears, have faith, and accept the good news. The kingdom of God has, indeed, come near.

Amen

Chavrusa

As I have proposed, Mark's Jewish context and Jewish points of view and sensibilities are valuable and important to try to understand his gospel. If I have succeeded in piquing your interest, gentle reader, and you wish to engage with others about what Mark has to say, let me suggest a typically Jewish approach: questions to consider, debate and, if possible, resolve. This would be a form of *chavrusa* learning, a traditional rabbinic approach to Talmudic study in which a small group of students (usually two-to-five) analyze, discuss, and debate a shared text. *Chavrusa* (also called *chavruta* or *havruta*) comes from Aramaic and means fellowship, friendship, companionship. In the spirit of *chavrusa* and the Talmudic Method and inspired by Jesus's human role as a rabbi, therefore, I offer a series of questions prompted by Mark's Gospel to spark discussion and refine and deepen understanding.

Chapter 1—The Headlines

- If the "kingdom of God" has come near, what is implied by the term "kingdom?"
- Why would Jesus call as his first followers tradesmen—working men? Why didn't he call religious leaders or, at least, individuals learned in the Torah?
- If Jesus said "Follow me" to you, what would you do? Isn't that what Mark's Gospel is asking of you? What do you say?
- Why does Jesus's mission begin in Galilee—a remote and unsophisticated province—and not Jerusalem or, at least, Judea?

Chapter 2—The Conflict Begins

- What does Jesus mean by "the Son of Man?" Is it different from "Son of God?" If so, how?
- The Nicene Creed tells us that Jesus was made man. As a man—a human being—what was Jesus like? What is your impression of him?

Chapter 3—Unclean Spirits and True Kindred

- What are unclean spirits?
- You are a respectable, upstanding member of the community who believes in God, tries to keep His Commandments, and complies with the practices that Moses directed: How do you react to Jesus?
- Why did Jesus reject his natural family?

Chapter 4—Teaching

- Are the parables—the sower, the measures, the farmer, the mustard seed—"good news?"
- In the face of great danger, is it wrong to be afraid?

Chapter 5—Healing

- Why did Jesus reach out to Gentiles? What does this imply about Judaism's relationship with, and responsibility to, Gentiles?
- Are humor and laughter part of Jesus's mission?

Chapter 6—Reprise

- Why doesn't Mark tell us about Jesus's birth and more about his origins?
- Why could Jesus "do no deed of power" in his hometown?

Chapter 7—Gentiles

- Who represents Jews and Judaism in Mark?
- What does Jesus think of Jews? Of Gentiles?

Chapter 8—The Big Reveal

- Three difficult boat trips and two feedings of loaves and fishes—metaphors or facts? Either way, what does the repetition tell us?
- What does a sign from heaven look like?
- Was Peter wrong to rebuke Jesus?
- Why were the disciples to wait to proclaim Jesus as the Messiah?

Chapter 9—Getting Ready

- Why, at crucial moments like the trip up the mountain and the encounter with Elijah and Moses, does Jesus choose an inner circle of Peter, James, and John?
- Peter et al., saw Elijah and Moses and heard the voice of God proclaiming Jesus as His son. Yet, on the road to Capernaum where Jesus tells them and the others that he is going to die and rise from the dead, they don't understand what Jesus is talking about. Why don't they get it? To be fair, perhaps we should ask ourselves: Do we?

Chapter 10—On to Jerusalem

- What does "Son of David" imply about Jesus? How does it relate to Son of God and Son of Man?
- Jesus has several things to say about marriage. Western law and culture in the twenty-first century don't agree with him. Do you? If not, why not?

Chapter 11—Jerusalem: Throwing the Gauntlet

- Was Jesus's entry into Jerusalem an act of humility or an assertion of kingship? If the latter, what kind of kingship was he asserting?
- Why did Jesus pick a fight with the temple religious authorities?
- What was the nature of the authority that Jesus and the temple religious leaders were disputing?

Chapter 12—Jerusalem: Routing the Establishment

- Why did the temple authorities believe that Jesus had to be stopped?
- Were any of their reasons understandable, even if ultimately wrong?

Chapter 13—Jerusalem: The Shape of Things to Come

- Why an inner circle of Peter, Andrew, James, and John for Jesus's eschatological predictions?
- What is the "desolating sacrilege" that will be "set up where it ought not to be?"
- How do we understand, and reconcile, the timing of what Jesus predicted?
- How is his reference to an "elect" consistent with his teaching in the parables about choices and admonitions about faith?

Chapter 14—Jerusalem: Passover

- Why did Jesus choose Passover as the key moment leading to his crucifixion and resurrection?
- Given Jesus's teachings about servanthood and first and last, why did he (and Mark) give bombastic, extroverted, assertive Peter particular attention?
- In view of Jesus's confession that he is the Messiah to the Chief Priest, does Judas get a bad rap?

Chapter 15—Jerusalem: Death

- Who killed Jesus?

Chapter 16—Resurrection

- Does the end of Mark's Gospel leave us with fear or faith?
- If faith, are we ready to follow Jesus?

Afterword—For Additional Study

As I NOTED IN my introduction, this commentary is based upon my own close reading of the Gospel of Mark. I utilized the New Revised Standard Version (NRSV) since it is the Bible translation used in the Episcopal Churches that I attend in Maryland and Florida. While I was sure that there were many commentaries on and analyses of Mark, I did not wish to have them affect my interpretation as my principal goal was to engage the text in a manner similar to the original readers of this, the oldest gospel.

Once I completed my commentary, I did want to see what other authoritative commentators had to say, and you may also. I found three that come at Mark from different perspectives and that are thought-provoking and useful. They are Joel Marcus, *The Anchor Yale Bible, Mark 1–8, Mark 8–16* (Yale University Press 2000), N.T.Wright, *Mark For Everyone* (Society for Promoting Christian Knowledge & John Knox Press 2004), and Larry Parsley, *An Easy Stroll Through a Short Gospel* (Mockingbird 2018). Marcus's work is a two-volume treatise aimed mainly at theology scholars and students. Wright's book is an Anglican bishop's homiletic consideration of the text. Parsley's book is a pastor's reflections written by a believer mainly for believers. It is beyond the scope of my commentary to analyze and critique what these distinguished authors have to say. But I can offer some comments that may help frame these works as you decide whether and how to delve further into Mark.

One issue common to all three concerns translation. If nothing else, I hope the reader will agree that I have been attentive to the text of Mark. However, that begs the question of which text? I have explained my choice of the NRSV, but there are of course many different translations of the Bible. And, in fact, both Marcus and Wright offer their own translations of Mark. Parsley uses the New International Version (NIV). As Rev. Dave Marshall, the Rector of All Angels By the Sea on Longboat Key, Florida, has pointed out, translation *is* interpretation. Differing translations can convey different emphases, shadings, and meanings.

An example—a very important one—involves the first quoted words of Jesus in the first chapter of Mark (1:14–15). As I have contended, these summarize Jesus's core message: "The time is fulfilled, and the kingdom of God has come near; repent, and believe in the good news." I consider this passage among the most important things that Jesus has to say—perhaps *the* most important. Here is the text of these first words of Jesus used by each of the three commentators:

- Marcus: "The time has been fulfilled, and the dominion of God has come near! Repent, and believe in the good news!"
- Wright: "The time is fulfilled! God's kingdom is arriving! Turn back, and believe the good news!"
- Parsley: "The time has come. The kingdom of God has come near. Repent and believe the good news."

The three versions are similar, but there are differences. Marcus's text calls what is coming the "dominion" of God, while Wright, Parsley, and the NRSV describe it as the "kingdom" of God. Another difference concerns "repent." Wright uses "turn back" instead of "repent," and contends that it reflects the view of the Old Testament, John the Baptist, and Jesus that Israel must first return to God. Still another take on "repent" is noted by Marcus. The Gospel of Mark was written in Greek, and the applicable Greek word was *metanoia*. This literally means "change of mind." Rev. Marshall, to whom I referred above, has contended that the sense in Greek was to raise one's thinking or, as we might put it in our time, to think outside the box. While still employing "repent," Marcus agrees that it reflects more than regret for individual acts, is deepened by the Jewish concept of "turning" and "return," and

Afterword—For Additional Study

implies a total change of spiritual orientation. Finally, Marcus and especially Wright use exclamation points; Parsley and the NRSV do not. The Marcus and Wright versions thereby convey a sense of greater urgency and excitement (with which I agree).

The nature of these three works will likely dictate how readers can most usefully employ them. Again, Marcus provides a full-scale treatise. It is two volumes and 1,181 pages. It begins with an introduction that consists of five essays on the Author, the Markan Community, Gospel Relationships, Markan Composition, and the Place of Mark in Christian Life and Thought. He groups the gospel into what he considers its major sections, and as noted above, offers his own translation. In each section, Marcus provides notes and comment. The notes explain the choices made in the translation, highlight exegetical problems, and convey technical information. Marcus considers the comment section as the heart of his work. He wants readers to focus on this, "from the pastor trying to get a 'fix' on a particular passage for a Sunday sermon to the professional scholar attempting to situate it within the development of early Christian life and thought." This indicates for whom Marcus's work was principally intended—those with substantial existing knowledge and sophistication in Christianity. The readers to whom I have addressed my commentary may thus find Marcus best used as a rich resource to be dipped into as need and curiosity demand.

Wright and Parsley aim for a broader audience, and their books are significantly shorter than Marcus's. They are both clergymen—Wright was the Bishop of Durham in the Church of England, and Parsley was Senior Pastor of Valley Ranch Baptist Church in Texas. Both are now in academia—Wright at Oxford and Parsley at Baylor. Wright's book, in its very title, says that it is "for everyone," and he succeeds in making many relatable and stimulating observations to a contemporary audience. Parsley similarly says that he writes no matter how one self-identifies when it comes to Jesus, and even asserts that he writes for those "outside the Christian fold." But almost immediately, he says that he envisions his reader as the "thirteenth disciple." And each short section of his book, commenting on passages from Mark, closes

Afterword—For Additional Study

with a short sentence reverently addressing Jesus as King, Messiah, and Son of God. (E.g., "Jesus, enfold the meandering plot of my life into the good news story you are writing," "Jesus, you are our gateway to the Father's blessing," "Jesus, your grace redeems my drivenness.") Parsley's "Mediations on Mark" thus assumes the conclusion toward which Mark was arguing and, I would contend, does not engage the gospel on its own terms. Nevertheless, both Wright and Parsley—and undoubtedly other sources—can profitably be consulted as one wrestles with Mark's "executive summary."

www.ingramcontent.com/pod-product-compliance
Lightning Source LLC
LaVergne TN
LVHW051705080426
835511LV00017B/2744